Culinary Math

Culinary Math

Linda Blocker + Julia Hill

THE CULINARY INSTITUTE OF AMERICA

John Wiley & Sons, Inc.

All interior photography by Lorna Smith.

CIA EDITORIAL TEAM:
Tim Ryan, Executive Vice President
Dr. Fred Mayo, Associate Vice President
Victor Gielisse, Associate Vice President and Dean, Culinary, Baking and Pastry Studies
Kathleen Zraly, Dean Liberal and Management Studies
Mary Cowell, Editorial Director
Mary Donovan, Senior Editor
Jessica Bard, Photo Editor
Lisa Lahey, Editor/Writer
Lorna Smith, Photographer
Elizabeth Corbett Johnson, Photo Studio Manager

This book is printed on acid-free paper. ♾

Published by John Wiley & Sons, Inc., New York.

Published simultaneously in Canada.

This publication is designed to provide accurate and authoritative information in regard to the subject matter covered. It is sold with the understanding that the publisher is not engaged in rendering professional services. If professional advice or other expert assistance is required, the services of a competent professional person should be sought.

Design by Vertigo Design, NYC

Library of Congress Cataloging-in-Publication Data:
Blocker, Linda.
    Culinary math / by Linda Blocker, Julia Hill [and] the Culinary Institute of America.
     p. cm.
    Includes index.
    ISBN 0-471-38740-1 (pbk. : acid-free paper)
Cookery-Mathemitics. I. Hill, Julie, 1954- II. Culinary Institute of America. III. Title.

TX652.B5844 2002
641.5'01'51-dc21   2001024344

Printed in the United States of America.

10 9 8 7 6 5 4 3

This book is dedicated to the wonderful people
in my life who have truly inspired me:
My husband Dr. Seth Blocker
My parents Arnold and Roslyn Weiss
My grandmother Freda Weiss
And in memory of my grandfather Robert Weiss
and my grandmother Jean Friedlander

—LB

To my husband and daughter, John and Keely Campbell

—JHH

We would also like to dedicate this book to our colleagues,
our friends, and our students who found success in this
math, perhaps for the first time!

We would like to extend our gratitude to the people
who helped make this project a reality: Mary Cowell, Susan
Wysocki, Bonnie Bogush, John Storm, Cathy Powers,
Anthony Ligouri, Victor Gielisse, and Ezra Eichelberger.

Contents

Preface

You are about to embark on a wonderful journey that links the world of mathematics to the culinary profession. Cooking has been referred to as an art; yet if you are creating your art with the intention of making a living, you need to apply some of the math fundamentals discussed in this text to be successful. The purpose of this book is to guide you in understanding and appropriately using the math of the food service industry.

Organization of the Book

AT THE END of the journey through this textbook you should feel confident costing out recipes, converting recipe sizes, and working with kitchen ratios. Each individual chapter is designed to move toward these goals one step at a time. These chapters build on one another, so it is important to be comfortable with the material covered in earlier chapters to be successful with the later material.

Chapter 1 reviews the basic math necessary to be able to successfully master the math in the remaining chapters.

Chapter 2 covers the units of measure used in most of the professional kitchens in the United States. It is very important to commit these units of measure and their conversions to memory to be able to work efficiently in the kitchen.

Chapters 3 and 4 cover converting units of measure within weight and volume, and Chapter 5 discusses converting between weight and volume measures.

Chapter 6 presents the concept of yield percentage and how it is calculated.

Chapters 7 and 8 examine how to calculate the cost and the edible-portion cost, and Chapter 9 combines these concepts in recipe costing.

Chapter 10 addresses how to use yield percent to determine how much of a product is usable and how to order the correct amount of a product for a particular need.

Chapter 11 is dedicated to special topics—situations that are exceptions to the rules covered in Chapters 6 through 10—and will cover how to identify these unique circumstances and formulate the math to find the solutions.

Chapter 12 deals with changing the yield of a recipe.

Chapter 13 introduces kitchen ratios, which are ratios that are specific to the food service industry.

Chapter 14 is dedicated to the metric system and explores how to convert these units to standard U.S. measure and vice versa as well as the areas of food service that use metric units.

Chapter 15 is a review chapter. This chapter consists of problems that test your understanding of the material covered in the text.

Organization of Each Chapter

EACH CHAPTER begins with a short vignette describing a situation that may be encountered in the food service industry, which connects the math in the chapter with a real-world application.

The chapter goals make you aware of the material to be covered in the chapter so that you can be sure you have met these goals.

Each chapter includes a lesson with example problems designed to show a method for solving a given problem. The procedures that are demonstrated reflect tried-and-true methods that have been presented successfully for the last fifteen years at the Culinary Institute of America; however, there are usually several ways to solve a problem, and if you perform different calculations and your solution matches the answer in the book, then you are probably on the right track.

At the end of each chapter there are practice problems for you to do on your own. Answers are listed at the end of the book for all of these problems so that you may check your calculations and gauge your understanding of the material.

How Best to Use the Practice Problems

ALL OF THE WORK for the practice problems should be shown so that errors may be easily seen and learned from. When all the work is done in your calculator, there will be no way to backtrack and find errors, which can be a very effective learning tool. Without the calculations on paper, you will know only that the answer is incorrect, not why it is wrong, which is the most important aspect of doing these problems. The correct answers for all the problems are provided for you in the back of the book.

Math that is connected to the real world of the culinary field is both challenging and rewarding. Do not forget to use common sense when reading through the chapters and example problems and doing the practice problems.

IN THIS BUSY KITCHEN a final check of the plates is being made prior to service to the guests. The uniformity of the plates demonstrates adherence to not only the principles of good presentation but also portion control, an essential in controlling costs. The professionals in this kitchen made certain that the serving sizes were correctly measured. Uniformity in portions and the correct number of portions can be calculated by these pro-

fessionals only if they employ the basics of culinary math. From ordering the ingredients for each dish to calculating the yield, the fundamentals of math played a key role in this successful operation.

Culinary Math

CHAPTER 1

Math Basics

The primary goal of this chapter is to review basic math, including whole numbers, fractions, and decimals. After completing the basic review, the chapter will cover percentages and then word problems and their solutions. This chapter is designed to be a resource that may be used as a reference for the subsequent chapters.

◾ USEFUL BASIC MATH TERMS

DECIMAL: a number that uses a decimal point and place value to show values less than one

DENOMINATOR: the "bottom" number in a fraction

DIVIDEND: the number to be divided in a division problem

DIVISOR: the number that the dividend is being divided by

FRACTION: a number symbolic of the relationship between the part and the whole that has a numerator and a denominator

IMPROPER FRACTION: a fraction with a numerator that is greater than or equal to the denominator, such as:

$$\frac{4}{3}$$

(continued)

goals

- Identify the place value of a whole number
- Convert a whole number to a fraction
- Identify the types of fractions
- Convert a mixed number to an improper fraction
- Convert fractions to decimals and decimals to fractions
- Solve an equation with fractions and decimals
- Convert a percentage to a decimal or fraction and a decimal or fraction to a percentage
- Solve word problems for the part, whole, or percent

LOWEST TERM FRACTION: the result of reducing a fraction so that the numerator and the denominator no longer have any common factors.

For example: $\dfrac{14}{28}$

Both 14 and 28 share the following factors: 2, 7, and 14. If you divide both 14 and 28 by the largest factor, 14, the result will be 1/2 which is equivalent to 14/28.

MIXED NUMBER: a number that contains both a whole number and a fraction, such as:

$$4\tfrac{1}{4}$$

MULTIPLICAND AND MULTIPLIER: the numbers being multiplied

NUMERATOR: the "top" number in a fraction

PERCENTAGE: a ratio of a number to 100; the symbol for percentage is %.

PRODUCT: the answer to a multiplication problem

PROPER FRACTION: a fraction in which the numerator is less than the denominator, such as:

 $\dfrac{2}{5}$

QUOTIENT: the answer to a division problem

RATIO: a comparison of two numbers or the quotient of two numbers. A ratio can be expressed as a fraction, a division problem or an expression, such as:

3/5, 3÷5, or 3 to 5

REMAINDER: the number that remains after dividing

REPEATING DECIMAL OR RECURRING DECIMAL: the result of converting a fraction to a decimal that repeats. If you convert 1/3 to a decimal the result is 0.3333333 . . . a repeating decimal (the '3' goes on infinitely). To record a repeating decimal, it is common to put a bar over the first set of repeating digits - .3

Whole Numbers

Place Values

The chart below identifies the place value of whole numbers.

WHOLE NUMBERS														
TRILLIONS			**BILLIONS**			**MILLIONS**			**THOUSANDS**			**UNITS**		
hundreds	tens	ones	hundreds	tens	ones	hundreds	tens	ones	hundreds	tens	ones	hundreds	tens	ones
__	__	__ ,	__	__	__ ,	__	__	__ ,	__	__	__ ,	__	__	__ .

It is important to be familiar with place value when dealing with whole-number operations.

Fractions

FRACTIONS ARE FREQUENTLY used in the kitchen. Measuring cups, measuring spoons, and the volumes and weights of products ordered may be expressed in fractional quantities. Most recipes or formulas found in a kitchen or in a cookbook deal with fractions. The fractions used in the kitchen are, for the most part, the more common fractions: 1/8, 1/4, 1/3, 1/2, 2/3, 3/4. A culinary recipe or formula would most likely never use a fraction such as 349/940 cups of flour.

A fraction may be thought of as:

- A part of a whole number: 3 out of 5 slices of pie could be represented as 3/5. In this example, 3 is the part and 5 is the whole.
- An expression of a relationship between two numbers

  $\dfrac{3}{7}$ The *numerator*, or top number
  The *denominator*, or bottom number

- A division problem: The fraction 3/7 can also be written as the division problem 3 ÷ 7.

Types of Fractions

Proper (Common) Fractions

In a proper or common fraction, the denominator is greater than the numerator.

$$\frac{1}{2} \text{ and } \frac{3}{4}$$

Improper Fractions

In an improper fraction, the numerator is greater than the denominator.

$$\frac{28}{7} \text{ and } \frac{140}{70}$$

Mixed Numbers

A mixed number is a whole number with a fraction.

$$4\frac{3}{8}$$

Converting Fractions

Converting Whole Numbers to Fractions

To convert a whole number to a fraction, place the whole number over 1.

Example: $5 \rightarrow \dfrac{5}{1}$

Converting Improper Fractions to Mixed Numbers

To convert an improper fraction to a mixed number, divide the numerator by the denominator. The quotient will be the whole number, and the remainder (if any) will be placed over the denominator of the original improper fraction to form the fractional part of the mixed number.

Example:

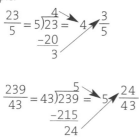

Warning

Remember that when dividing, the numerator is the number being divided.

Numerator ÷ Denominator

or

Denominator)‾Numerator

Converting Mixed Numbers to Improper Fractions

Follow these steps to convert a mixed number to an improper fraction.

1. Multiply the whole number by the denominator.

2. Add the result to the numerator.

3. Place the resulting number over the original denominator.

Example: Convert 4 2/3 to an improper fraction.

step 1: Multiply 4 and 3. $4\frac{2}{3}$ $4 \times 3 = 12$

step 2: Add 2 to the result. $4\frac{2}{3}$ $12 + 2 = 14$

step 3: Use 14 from step 2 as the numerator and 3 as the denominator.

$$\frac{14}{3} = 4\frac{2}{3}$$

Note that the denominator is the same in both the improper fraction and the mixed number.

Addition of Fractions

Fractions that are added to one another must have the same denominator (common denominator).

Example:

$$\frac{1}{7} + \frac{2}{7} = \frac{3}{7}$$

7 is the common denominator.

Example: Solve $\frac{5}{7} + \frac{1}{4}$

To solve this example, first a common denominator must be found. Here are two methods.

1. *Multiply the two denominators together.*

    To find the common denominator for 5/7 and 1/4, multiply the first denominator, 7, by the second denominator, 4: $(7 \times 4) = 28$. The numerator of each fraction must be multiplied by the same number as the denominator was multiplied by, so that the value of the fraction remains the same. In this example, multiply the 5 by 4, and multiply the 1 by 7.

Thus: $\dfrac{5}{7} = \dfrac{5 \times 4}{7 \times 4} = \dfrac{20}{28}$

$\dfrac{1}{4} = \dfrac{1 \times 7}{4 \times 7} = \dfrac{7}{28}$

$\dfrac{20}{28} + \dfrac{7}{28} = \dfrac{27}{28}$

2. *By inspection.*

Often a common denominator will be evident when a denominator of one fraction is evenly divisible by the denominator in the other fraction. In the following example, 16 can be divided by 8 so it can be used as the common denominator. This method can save time but will only work when one of the denominators is a factor of the other.

$$\dfrac{1}{8} + \dfrac{5}{16} = \dfrac{1 \times 2}{8 \times 2} + \dfrac{5 \times 1}{16 \times 1} = \dfrac{2}{16} + \dfrac{5}{16} = \dfrac{7}{16}$$

Subtraction of Fractions

Fractions that are subtracted from one another must also have a common denominator. The same mathematical rule used to convert denominators that are not the same to common denominators for the addition of fractions can be used when subtracting fractions.

Examples:

$$\dfrac{3}{8} - \dfrac{1}{8} = \dfrac{2}{8} = \dfrac{1}{4}$$

$$\dfrac{7}{8} - \dfrac{5}{9} = \dfrac{7 \times 9}{8 \times 9} - \dfrac{5 \times 8}{9 \times 8} = \dfrac{63}{72} - \dfrac{40}{72} = \dfrac{23}{72}$$

Multiplication of Fractions

The process of multiplying fractions simply requires that the numerators be multiplied and the result placed over the result of multiplying the denominators.

Any mixed numbers must first be converted to improper fractions before multiplying them.

$$\dfrac{\text{Numerator} \times \text{Numerator}}{\text{Denominator} \times \text{Denominator}} = \dfrac{NN}{DD}$$

Examples:

$$\dfrac{4}{7} \times \dfrac{3}{5} = \dfrac{12}{35}$$

$$1\dfrac{1}{2} \times \dfrac{1}{5} \times \dfrac{1}{7} = \dfrac{3}{2} \times \dfrac{1}{5} \times \dfrac{1}{7} = \dfrac{3}{70}$$

Division of Fractions

To divide fractions, first convert any mixed numbers to improper fractions. Next, invert the second fraction (the divisor) by placing the denominator on top of the numerator. Finally, change the division sign to a multiplication sign and complete the equation as a multiplication problem.

Examples: $\dfrac{3}{4} \div 1\dfrac{2}{3} = \dfrac{3}{4} \div \dfrac{5}{3} = \dfrac{3}{4} \times \dfrac{3}{5} = \dfrac{9}{20}$

$\dfrac{7}{1} \div \dfrac{3}{4} = \dfrac{7}{1} \times \dfrac{4}{3} = \dfrac{28}{3} = 9\dfrac{1}{3}$

Remember

A common denominator is **not required** when multiplying or dividing fractions.

Decimals

DECIMALS ARE a place value system based on the number 10. A decimal is the fractional part of a whole expressed in powers of 10. A point (.), called a decimal point, is used to indicate the decimal form of the number.

Place Values

The place values of the numbers to the right of the decimal are as follows:

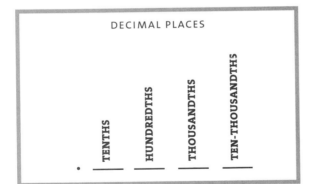

DECIMAL PLACES

TENTHS HUNDREDTHS THOUSANDTHS TEN-THOUSANDTHS

Examples:

$\dfrac{1}{10} = 0.1$

$\dfrac{9}{100} = 0.09$

$\dfrac{89}{1000} = 0.089$

$\dfrac{321}{10000} = 0.0321$

Addition and Subtraction of Decimals

The decimal points and place values must be aligned when adding and subtracting decimal values. For instance, if you are adding .14 and .5 it is important remember that you can only add numbers of the same place value. So, you must add the 1 to the 5 since they are both in the tenths place. The answer to this problem is .64 not .19.

Thus $3.14 + 18.4 + 340.1 + 200.147 =$

$$
\begin{array}{r}
3.14 \\
18.4 \\
340.1 \\
+200.147 \\
\hline
561.787
\end{array}
$$

and $9.736 - 6.5 =$

$$
\begin{array}{r}
9.736 \\
-6.5 \\
\hline
3.236
\end{array}
$$

Multiplication of Decimals

$$
\begin{array}{r}
\text{Multiplicand} \\
\times \text{Multiplier} \\
\hline
\text{Product}
\end{array}
$$

First, multiply decimals as though they were whole numbers. Then mark off from right to left the same number of decimal places as found in both the multiplier and multiplicand (number multiplied) and place the point in your answer (the product).

Example: $40.8 \times 3.02 =$ $40.8 = 1$ decimal place
$$
\begin{array}{r}
\times 3.02 = 2 \text{ decimal places} \\
\hline
816 \\
+ 122400 \\
\hline
123.216 = 3 \text{ decimal places}
\end{array}
$$

Division of Decimals

$$
\begin{array}{r}
\text{QUOTIENT} \\
\hline
\text{DIVISOR)DIVIDEND}
\end{array}
$$

To divide decimals:

1. Set up the division problem as you would if you were dividing whole numbers.

2. Move the decimal point of the divisor to the right (if it is not already a whole number) so that you have a whole number. This will eliminate any decimal in the divisor.

3. Move the decimal point in the dividend the same number of places to the right. If you need to move the decimal more places than there are digits, add zeros to accommodate this move.

4. Place another decimal point right above the decimal's new position in the dividend. This places the decimal point in your answer (quotient).

5. Divide as though you are dividing whole numbers – disregarding the decimal points. Be careful to keep the digits in the same place values lined up as you divide. For the purposes of this text, dividing to the ten-thousandths place is sufficient.

Examples: $8.325 \div 2.25 =$

$$
\begin{array}{r}
3.7 \\
225\overline{)832.5} \\
\underline{675} \\
1575 \\
\underline{1575} \\
0
\end{array}
$$

$$12 \div 1.5 =$$

$$
\begin{array}{r}
8 \\
1.5\overline{)12.0}
\end{array}
$$

Converting Fractions to Decimals

To convert any fraction to its equivalent decimal fraction, carry out the division.

Example: Convert $\frac{1}{2}$ to decimal form: $2\overline{)1.0}^{.5}$

Converting Decimals to Fractions

To convert a decimal number to a fraction:

1. Read the number as a decimal using place value.

2. Write the number as a fraction.

3. Reduce to lowest terms.

Example: Convert .0075 to a fraction.
1. Seventy-five ten-thousandths.

2. $\dfrac{75}{10000}$

3. $\dfrac{75}{10000} = \dfrac{3}{400}$

Percentages

THE TERM *PERCENT* means "part of a hundred"; thus 7 percent means 7 parts out of every 100. If 34 percent of the customers in a restaurant favor nutritious entrées, a part of a whole number of customers is being expressed. The whole is represented by 100 percent. In this example, all of the customers that enter the restaurant represent 100 percent.

The use of percentages to express a rate is common practice in the food-service industry. For example, food and beverage costs, labor costs, operating costs, fixed costs, and profits are usually stated as a percentage to establish standards of control.

To indicate that any number is a percentage, the number must be accompanied by a percent sign (%).

Converting Decimals to Percentages

To convert any decimal to a percentage, multiply the number by 100 and add a percent sign.

Example: $.25 = .25 \times 100 = 25\%$
A shortcut would be to simply move the decimal point two places to the right and add a percentage sign.

Converting Percentages to Decimals

To convert percentages to decimal form, divide by 100 and drop the percent sign.

> **Remember**
>
> Any time you use percentages in a mathematical operation—in a calculator, with a pencil and paper, or in your head— you must first convert the percentage to its decimal equivalent.

Example: $30\% = \dfrac{30}{100} = .30$

A shortcut would be to simply move the decimal point two places to the left and drop the percent sign.

If there is a fraction in the percentage, first change that fraction to a decimal.

For example: $37\dfrac{1}{4}\%$

$$37\dfrac{1}{4}\% = 37.25\%$$

$$37.25\% \rightarrow .3725$$

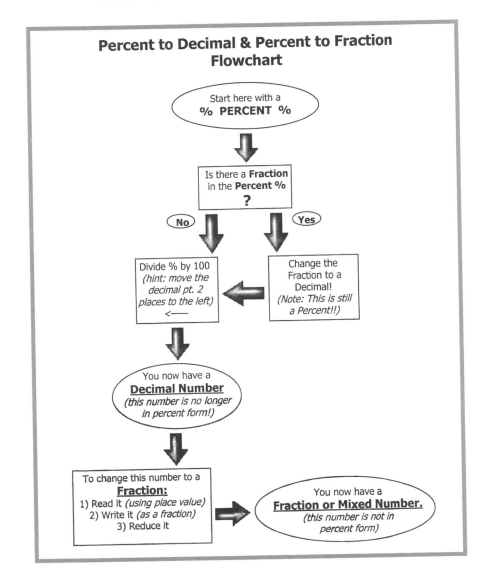

Percent to Decimal & Percent to Fraction Flowchart

Start here with a
% PERCENT %

Is there a **Fraction** in the **Percent %** **?**

No

Yes

Divide % by 100
(hint: move the decimal pt. 2 places to the left)
←——

Change the Fraction to a Decimal!
(Note: This is still a Percent!!)

You now have a
Decimal Number
(this number is no longer in percent form!)

To change this number to a
Fraction:
1) Read it *(using place value)*
2) Write it *(as a fraction)*
3) Reduce it

You now have a
Fraction or Mixed Number.
(this number is not in percent form)

Percentages in the Kitchen

In the kitchen it is often necessary for the chef to work with percentages. Chefs may use percentages to calculate and apply a yield percentage or food cost percentage. In these cases it is helpful to remember the following formulas.

$$\text{Percent} = \frac{\text{Part}}{\text{Whole}}$$

$$\text{Part} = \text{Whole} \times \text{Percent}$$

$$\text{Whole} = \frac{\text{Part}}{\text{Percent}}$$

Hints for using formulas involving percentages:

- The number or word that follows the word *of* is usually the whole number and the word *is* usually is connected to the part. What is 20% of 70? In this example, "of" 70 implies that 70 is the whole. 20% is the percentage. What "is" implies that the part is the unknown and what you are solving for.
- The percentage will always be identified with either the symbol % or the word *percent*.
- The part will usually be less than the whole.

The Percentage Triangle

The following triangle is a tool used to find part, whole, or percentage.

Directions for Using the Percentage Triangle

1. Determine what you are looking for—part, whole, or percentage.

2. *To find the part:*
   Cover the P for part.
   W and % are side by side. This directs you to multiply the whole by the percentage. (Remember to first change the percentage to a decimal by dividing by 100.)

   To find the whole:
   Cover the W for whole.
   P is over %. This directs you to divide the part by the percentage.
   (Remember to first change the percentage to a decimal by dividing by 100.)

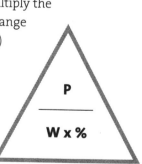

   To find the percentage:
   Cover the % for percentage.
   P is over W. This directs you to divide the part by the whole and multiply the answer by 100 to convert it to the percentage.

Solving Word Problems

WORD PROBLEMS ARE good practice for applied math because they use real-life situations. Below is a list of steps designed to break down the process of solving word problems into manageable pieces.

THE FIVE STEPS TO SOLVING WORD PROBLEMS

step 1: Determine what is being solved for.

step 2: Decide what must be done to get the answer.

step 3: Perform the necessary calculations.

step 4: Find out if the question has been answered by the calculations.

step 5: Decide whether the answer is reasonable.

Step 5, determining if an answer is reasonable, takes on a whole new meaning in culinary math, which is related to real situations dealing with food. For instance, a problem could ask how many apple pies should be made for dinner if 40 percent of your customers usually order a slice of apple pie. Each pie is cut into 8 slices, and you are expecting 240 customers this evening. After you complete the calculations, your answer indicates that you need 240 pies. At this point you should ask yourself if this answer makes sense given the other information you have. If you are expecting 240 customers, this would mean that the number you arrived at allows for one pie per person; clearly something is wrong with the calculations. When this occurs, you should go over your work to find where the error was made. The ability to find errors will indicate a clear understanding of the concept and facilitate your learning.

Conclusion

BASIC MATH IS THE FOUNDATION for all of the math covered in this text. Understanding the concepts covered is the key to your success in *Culinary Math*. You should refer back to this chapter as you progress through the book if needed.

Chapter in Review

1. Calculate the following:

A. $\dfrac{1}{2} + \dfrac{1}{8} =$ **B.** $\dfrac{1}{6} + \dfrac{1}{5} =$ **C.** $6\dfrac{1}{6} + \dfrac{1}{4} =$

D. $\dfrac{2}{3} + \dfrac{3}{4} =$ **E.** $10 + \dfrac{1}{9} + \dfrac{2}{3} =$ **F.** $\dfrac{2}{10} - \dfrac{1}{6} =$

G. $\dfrac{1}{2} + \dfrac{1}{8} =$ **H.** $7\dfrac{3}{8} - \dfrac{2}{24} =$ **I.** $\dfrac{5}{6} \times \dfrac{2}{3} =$

J. $15 \times \dfrac{4}{5} =$ **K.** $1\dfrac{3}{4} \times 4\dfrac{3}{8} =$ **L.** $\dfrac{\frac{1}{2}}{\frac{1}{4}} =$

M. $\dfrac{1}{4} \div \dfrac{7}{8} =$ **N.** $1\dfrac{1}{2} \div 6 =$ **O.** $1\dfrac{3}{8} \div 6\dfrac{7}{10} =$

2. Is the answer reasonable? Complete the following chart.

QUESTION	ANSWER	UNREASONABLE BECAUSE:	ANSWER SHOULD BE APPROXIMATELY:
A. What is your salary per month for your full-time job?	$32.41		
B. You have 3 pints of strawberries. Each cake requires 1 1/2 pints. How many cakes did you make?	6 cakes		
C. You have 20 pounds of dough. Each loaf requires 3/4 pound of dough. How many loaves can you make?	2 loaves		
D. How much do you pay in rent each month?	$32.50		
E. How many customers did you serve last night?	2,399,001		
F. What is the check average in your restaurant?	$.29		
G. How many total hours did the dishwasher work this week?	168 hours		

3. Convert the following fractions into their decimal equivalent.

Example: $\frac{1}{2} = .5$

A. $\frac{3}{2}$

B. $\frac{3}{8}$

C. $\frac{9}{18}$

D. $\frac{5}{16}$

E. $\frac{2}{5}$

F. $\frac{7}{8}$

G. $\frac{6}{24}$

H. $\frac{3}{48}$

I. $\frac{26}{5}$

J. $\frac{66}{10}$

K. $\frac{440}{100}$

L. $\frac{4400}{1000}$

4. Solve the following. If your answer has more than four decimal places, drop all digits past four places . Do not round the answer.

A. $3.6024 + 18.32 + 51.05 + 2.5 =$

B. $0.0365 + 0.001 + 0.999 =$

C. $9.765 - 4.0631 =$

D. $1.2634 - 0.99 =$

E. $78 \div 0.0347 =$

F. $0.025 \div 98.75 =$

G. $91.30 \div 40 =$

H. $0.32 \times 1.10 =$

I. $0.065 \times 2.001 =$

J. $42 \times 1.5 =$

5. Find the decimal equivalent for the following:

A. 7285%

B. 9.99%

C. $\frac{1}{4}$%

D. 100%

E. 0.5%

F. 25%

6. Change these numbers to percentages.

    A. 0.0125   **B.** 9.99   **C.** 0.00001

    D. $\dfrac{2}{5}$ **E.** $1\dfrac{1}{8}$

7. The bakeshop has an order for 10 dozen rolls. Forty rolls have been baked. What percentage of the rolls still have to be baked?

8. Betty usually charges $.85 per piece for mini appetizers. For a large party she charges her customers $680 for a thousand mini appetizers. What percent discount was Betty offering?

9. A restaurant purchases 40 pounds of potatoes. Twenty percent of the potatoes are peels. How many pounds of potatoes are peels?

10. If you order 300 lobster tails and you use 32 percent, how many do you have left?

11. You made 400 rolls, which is 40 percent of what you have to make. What is the total number of rolls you have to make?

12. You have 60 percent of a bottle of raspberry syrup remaining. If 10 ounces were used, how many ounces did the bottle originally hold?

13. Out of 250 cakes you use 34 percent for a party. How many cakes are left over?

14. What percent discount would you have gotten if the actual price of an item was $16.95 and you paid $15.96?

15. Annual recycling costs are $7,000. Annual sales amount to $1,185,857. What percent of sales does recycling cost represent?

16. You have a bakeshop staff of 30, which is 20 percent of your total staff. How many members do you have in your total staff?

17. If a caterer receives an order for 2800 canapés at $.06 each and he requires 30 percent down, how much will the client owe after the deposit is paid?

18. A restaurant orders a box of mixed fruits that contains 64 pieces of fruit in all. The box contains 25 percent oranges, and the rest of the fruit is grapefruit. How many grapefruits are there in this box of mixed fruit?

19. Bob makes a pot of coffee. By 10 A.M. only 3 cups remain. If 85 percent of the coffee has been consumed, how many cups of coffee did the pot originally hold?

20. You are serving 3 different entrées at a party you are catering. If 100 guests are having beef, 175 guests are having pasta, and 45 percent of the guests are having chicken, how many guests are expected at this party?

21. A case of apples you received has 12 rotten apples in it. If this represents 25 percent of the entire case, how many apples were in the case?

22. Mr. Smith purchased $125.00 worth of spices and herbs. Because this was such a large order, the supplier charged Mr. Smith only $95.00. What percent discount did Mr. Smith receive?

23. You are serving a dinner party for 25 guests. Each guest will receive a ramekin of chocolate mousse. If only 18 guests show up, what percent of the mousse will be left over?

CHAPTER 2

Units of Measure

Volumes and Weights in the U.S. Kitchen

goals

- List the names and abbreviations of the units of measure most commonly used in the foodservice industry

- Demonstrate your understanding of the relative sizes of the measuring tools used in the foodservice industry

- Recall the equivalents of volume measures without references

- Recall the equivalents of weight measures without references

- Explain the difference between weight and volume measurements

- Define a fluid ounce and explain how it differs from an ounce

If you work in a kitchen, it is necessary to know the units of measure and the relationship between the units. Many of the of the measuring devices found in a kitchen may not have markings on them, and you will need to know the relative size of measuring containers to be able to identify one from the other. For instance, if a recipe calls for 1 quart of chicken stock, you need to be able to select the correct measuring container.

Imagine that you are working in a kitchen that is running behind in production ("in the weeds") for lunch. You are preparing cream of broccoli soup and need 3 quarts of chicken stock. The only measuring container available is a 1-gallon container. You are aware that there are 4 quarts in 1 gallon and, therefore, 3/4 of the container will equal 3 quarts. If you did not know this, you would have to take the additional time to look for a quart container and fill the quart measure three times.

Knowing the units of measure will allow you to solve these problems. As a professional in the foodservice industry, you will need to be very familiar with many different units of measure.

These are the most common pieces of measuring equipment used in a professional kitchen in the United States.

Nested measuring cups

NESTED MEASURING CUPS are used for dry ingredients. The common sizes are 1 cup, 1/2 cup, 1/3 cup, and 1/4 cup.

MEASURING SPOONS are used for dry and liquid ingredients. The common sizes are 1 tablespoon, 1 teaspoon, 1/2 teaspoon, and 1/4 teaspoon.

Measuring spoons

GRADUATED MEASURING CUPS may be made of plastic or aluminum and are usually used for measuring liquids. The common sizes are 1 cup, 1 pint, 1 quart, and 1 gallon.

Graduated measuring cups

LADLES are used for measuring liquid. The common sizes include 2 fluid ounces, 4 fluid ounces, and 8 fluid ounces.

Ladles

PORTION SCOOPS come in a wide variety of sizes and are used to regulate single portions of finished food rather than ingredients. The scoops are numbered, and each number corresponds to the number of scoops it would take to make a quart. For instance, a number 30 scoop means that there would be 30 scoops needed to make a quart. In this photograph a number 10 scoop, which holds 3.2 fluid ounces, a number 16 scoop, which holds 2 fluid ounces, and a number 30 scoop, which holds 1.06 fluid ounces, are shown.

Portion scoops

THE MOST COMMON SCALES to measure weight in a kitchen are the digital (electronic) scale, the balance beam scale, and the spring-loaded scale.

Common scales

COMMON FOODSERVICE MEASUREMENTS AND ABBREVIATIONS

COMMON TERM	ABBREVIATION
teaspoon	t, tsp
tablespoon	T, tbsp
cup	C, c
pint	pt
quart	qt
gallon	G, gal
peck	pk
bushel	BU
fluid ounce	fl oz
ounce	oz
pound	lb, #
each	ea
bunch	bu
to taste	tt

Volume

VOLUME MEASUREMENT, as it applies to the kitchen, generally refers to the common household measuring tools used in the United States, such as cups, teaspoons, and quarts. These tools are used to define the space that is filled with the products being measured. Volume measures are related to each other in a very specific way. For example, 1 cup of a substance is always equal to 16 tablespoons of the same substance, just as 1 tablespoon of a substance is always equal to 3 teaspoons of the same substance (see Figure 2.1).

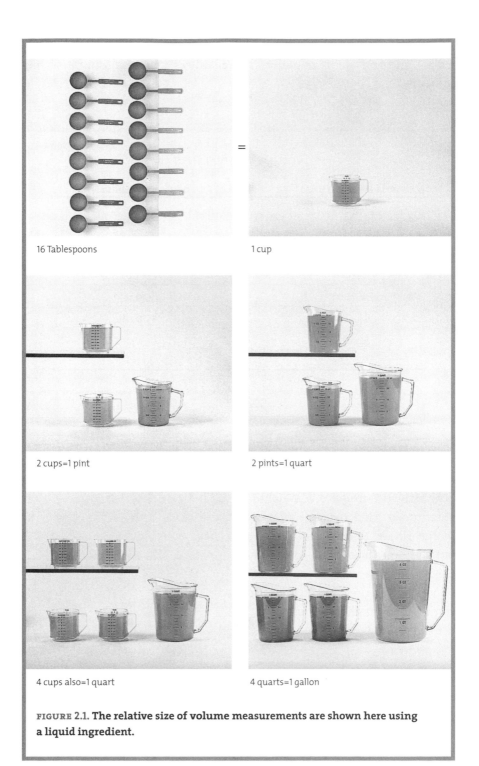

16 Tablespoons = 1 cup

2 cups=1 pint

2 pints=1 quart

4 cups also=1 quart

4 quarts=1 gallon

FIGURE 2.1. The relative size of volume measurements are shown here using a liquid ingredient.

The chart below shows units of volume measurement and their equivalents. These equivalents are always true regardless of what substance is being measured.

VOLUME EQUIVALENTS

VOLUME MEASURES	VOLUME EQUIVALENTS
1 teaspoon	—
1 tablespoon	3 teaspoons
1 cup	16 tablespoons
1 pint	2 cups
1 quart	2 pints
1 gallon	4 quarts
1 peck	2 gallons
1 bushel	4 pecks

Weight

IN CONTRAST TO VOLUME, weight is how heavy a substance is. Weight is determined using a scale. In kitchens in the United States there are two units of measure most commonly used to express weight: pounds and ounces (see Figure 2.2). You may also come across another unit of weight: the ton, which is 2,000 pounds.

WEIGHT EQUIVALENT

1 pound = 16 ounces

FIGURE 2.2. **Baking chocolate is often sold scored for measurement in 1-ounce blocks.**

The Ounce Confusion

Some recipes list quantities of ingredients by the fluid ounce, and many ingredients are purchased and packaged by the fluid ounce. Fluid ounces refer to volume, not weight. The chart below lists the volume equivalents for fluid ounces. It is important to be familiar with these facts.

ADDITIONAL VOLUME EQUIVALENTS

VOLUME MEASURE	EQUIVALENT IN FLUID OUNCES
1 tablespoon	1/2 fluid ounce
1 cup	8 fluid ounces
1 pint	16 fluid ounces
1 quart	32 fluid ounces
1 gallon	128 fluid ounces

Many people believe that 1 cup of an ingredient always weighs 8 ounces, no matter what is in the cup. In truth, only 1 cup (8 fluid ounces) of water or water-like liquids (liquids that have the same density as water) will assuredly weigh 8 ounces. If something other than water or a water-like liquid is measured in a cup, it will still equal 8 fluid ounces, but it will not necessarily weigh 8 ounces.

This confusion comes from not distinguishing the term *ounce* from the term *fluid ounce*. An ounce is something that you weigh, and a fluid ounce is a volume measure. The measurement for 1 fluid ounce is derived from the amount of space needed to hold a quantity of water weighing 1 ounce of water. Fluid ounces and ounces are the same only when the ingredient being measured has the same density as water.

Some examples of water-like liquids include alcohol, juices, vinegar, and oil (actually, oil is lighter than water, but the difference is so small that it is ignored in culinary applications). In instances such as these, the terms *fluid ounce* and *ounce* may be used interchangeably. On the contrary, when a recipe calls for a liquid such as honey, corn syrup, molasses, maple syrup, or heavy cream, you must pay close attention to the type of measure called for. One cup or 8 fluid ounces of any of these substances will not weigh 8 ounces (for example, 8 fluid ounces of honey weighs 12 ounces), and results will vary significantly if the terms are used interchangeably.

MANY PEOPLE MISTAKENLY use a ladle to measure ingredients in ounces. Ladles measure in fluid ounces. If a 4-fluid-ounce ladle (equivalent to 1/2 cup) was used to measure flour, the quantity in the ladle would weigh only about 2 ounces.

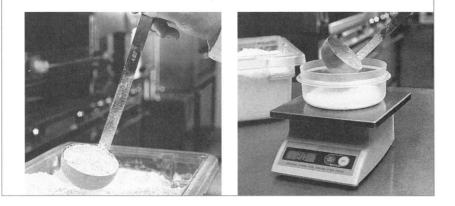

Conclusion

To WORK EFFICIENTLY in a kitchen and prepare products successfully, it is necessary to learn these skills. These are the measurements currently used in the majority of commercial kitchens in the United States. If you are planning to go anywhere else in the world to cook, you will also need to know the metric system (see Chapter 14).

We have gone to great lengths to explain the difference between fluid ounces and ounces, a unit of weight. Even manufacturers, when printing the measurements on measuring devices, will omit "fl" (the abbreviation for fluid) before the word "ounce" on an item clearly designed to measure fluid ounces. The culinary professional should use common sense and be alert.

IN THIS RECIPE FOR GUACAMOLE, 8 fluid ounces of scallions were called for in the recipe (see image on right). The chef mistakenly used 8 ounces by weight (see image on left). Which dip would you rather eat? It is important to note the difference in a recipe between fluid ounces and ounces by weight.

Chapter in Review

Tips on How to Memorize the Equivalents

1. Make flash cards using index cards or small pieces of paper and the table below to assist you.

MEASUREMENT STUDY CARDS

FRONT OF THE CARD	BACK OF THE CARD
1 tbsp = _____ tsp	1 tbsp = __3__ tsp
1 cup = _____ tbsp	1 cup = __16__ tbsp
1 cup = _____ tsp	1 cup = __48__ tsp
1 pt = _____ cups	1 pt = __2__ cups
1 qt = _____ pt	1 qt = __2__ pt
1 qt = _____ cups	1 qt = __4__ cups
1 gal = _____ qt	1 gal = __4__ qt
1 gal = _____ pt	1 gal = __8__ p
1 gal = _____ cups	1 gal = __16__ cups
1 bushel = _____ pecks	1 bushel = __4__ pecks
1 bushel = _____ gallons	1 bushel = __8__ gallons
1 peck = _____ gallons	1 peck = __2__ gallons
1 cup of water = _____ oz	1 cup of water = __8__ oz
1 quart of water = _____ oz	1 quart of water = __32__ oz
1 gal of water = _____ oz	1 gal of water = __128__ oz
1 tbsp of water = _____ oz	1 tbsp of water = __1/2__ oz
1 pound = _____ oz	1 pound = __16__ oz

2. Practice using the flash cards until you know the measurements and their equivalents quickly and without error. One way to do this is to make two piles: the ones you know and the ones that you do not know. Practice until all the cards are in the pile of the ones you know.

3. Study in groups. Using the flash cards, flip a card down onto the table; whoever says the equivalent first keeps the card. Quiz each other with the cards you have in your hand, because those will be the cards your study mates don't know as well as you do.

4. If you have access to an equipment storage room, become familiar with the measuring containers. Take out all of the measuring containers you can find. Fill the largest container with water and see how many times you can fill the smaller containers. You may also want to weigh a container filled with various ingredients on the scale. (Many people are visual learners and find it helpful to see the relationships between these measures.)

5. Use some study aids such as:

Study Questions

1. Discuss the difference between a weight measure and a volume measure.

2. A. What is the difference between 8 fluid ounces and 1 cup?

B. What is the difference between 8 ounces and 8 fluid ounces?

c. What is the difference between 1 cup and 8 ounces?

D. Complete the following table:

INGREDIENT:	WEIGHS 8 OZ IN A CUP?	HOW DO YOU KNOW THAT?	8 FL OZ IN A CUP?	HOW DO YOU KNOW THAT?
Water				
Molasses				
Flour				

3. Test yourself. In one minute or less complete the following:

A. 1 cup is equal to _____ tablespoons.

B. 1 bushel is equal to _____ pecks.

c. 1 tablespoon is equal to _____ teaspoons.

D. 1 pint is equal to _____ cups.

E. 1 gallon is equal to _____ quarts.

F. 1 quart is equal to _____ pints.

G. 1 peck is equal to _____ gallons.

H. 1 pound is equal to _____ ounces.

Use your knowledge of percentages (Chapter 1) for questions 4–10.

4. What percent of a gallon is a quart?

5. What percent of a tablespoon is a teaspoon?

6. A gallon is 50 percent of what measure?

7. A peck is 25 percent of what measure?

8. What percent of a cup is a tablespoon?

9. If you have 1 cup of flour and you use 4 tablespoons, what percent is left in the cup?

10. Six ounces of water is what percent of a quart?

11. If a recipe you are using called for 2 fluid ounces of flour, how much of a cup of flour should you use in the recipe?

12. In one minute or less answer the following:

    A. 1 quart is equal to _____ fluid ounces.

    B. 1 tablespoon is equal to _____ fluid ounce(s).

    C. 1 cup is equal to _____ fluid ounces.

    D. 1 pint is equal to _____ fluid ounces.

    E. 1 gallon is equal to _____ fluid ounces.

    F. If your friend said to you, "I have to use 8 ounces of parsley in a recipe. I'll just measure a cup of it, right?" what would you say?

13. Give an example (fact or fiction) of a situation that proves that it is imperative for you to know units of measure.

Basic Conversion of Units of Measure within Volume or Weight

- Demonstrate your understanding of the bridge method to convert units of measure within weight

- Demonstrate your understanding of the bridge method to convert units of measure within volume

You are making vegetable burgers, and the recipe calls for 36 ounces of ground walnuts. Walnuts are available from your supplier only in pound units. You must be able to calculate that 2 1/4 pounds is equivalent to 36 ounces so that you can place your order. Once you understand the units of measure and how they are related, you will be able to convert easily from one to the other. In this chapter we are going to investigate how to do unit conversions.

Converting Units of Measure: The Basics

How WOULD A CALCULATION such as converting 36 ounces to 2 1/4 pounds be done?

The bridge method is the "recipe" for converting from one unit of measure to another. It can be used to convert ounces to pounds, quarts to pints, tablespoons to cups, grams to ounces, volume to weight, and so on.

The bridge method is not the only method that can be used to make unit conversions. An alternative method or shortcut will be discussed at the end of this chapter.

A review page for the weight and volume equivalents from Chapter 2 has been provided for easy reference.

VOLUME MEASURES	VOLUME EQUIVALENTS
1 teaspoon	——
1 tablespoon	3 teaspoons
1 cup	16 tablespoons
1 pint	2 cups
1 quart	2 pints
1 gallon	4 quarts
1 peck	2 gallons
1 bushel	4 pecks

WEIGHT EQUIVALENT
1 pound = 16 ounces

Review of Weight and Volume Equivalents

Example: Convert 36 ounces to pounds.

step 1: If the unit of measurement that you are converting is a whole number, put it over 1. If it is a fraction, first convert it to a decimal and then put it over 1.

$$\frac{36 \text{ oz}}{1}$$

step 2: Place a multiplication sign next to this.

$$\frac{36 \text{ oz}}{1} \times$$

step 3: Draw another fraction line.

$$\frac{36 \text{ oz}}{1} \times \frac{\quad}{\quad}$$

step 4: Put in the units of measurement. The unit of measurement to be removed (ounces) is written on the bottom. The unit of to be converted to (pounds) is written on top.

$$\frac{36 \text{ oz}}{1} \times \frac{\text{lb}}{\text{oz}}$$

step 5: Enter the numbers to create the equivalency (1 pound = 16 ounces).

$$\frac{36\ oz}{1} \times \frac{1\ lb}{16\ oz}$$

step 6: Multiply straight across. Disregard the different units of measurement.

$$\frac{36\ oz}{1} \times \frac{1\ lb}{16\ oz} = \frac{36}{16}$$

step 7: Reduce the fraction answer if necessary.

$$\frac{36\ oz}{1} \times \frac{1\ lb}{16\ oz} = \frac{36}{16} = 2.25\ or\ 2\frac{1}{4}$$

step 8: Cancel like units of measurement and carry over the remaining unit of measurement to the answer.

$$\frac{36\ \cancel{oz}}{1} \times \frac{1\ lb}{16\ \cancel{oz}} = \frac{36}{16} = 2.25\ or\ 2\frac{1}{4}\ lbs$$

RECIPE FOR THE BRIDGE METHOD

INGREDIENTS

- Unit of measurement to be converted
- Unit of measurement to be converted to
- Equivalencies from Chapter 2

THE BRIDGE METHOD

step 1: If the unit of measurement that you are converting is a whole number, put it over 1. If it is a fraction, first convert it to a decimal and then put it over 1.

step 2: Place a multiplication sign next to this.

step 3: Draw another fraction line.

step 4: Put in the units of measurement. The unit of measurement to be removed is written on the bottom. The unit of measurement to be converted to is written on the top.

step 5: Enter the numbers to create the equivalency.

step 6: Multiply straight across, disregarding the different units of measurement.

step 7: Reduce the resulting fraction (if necessary).

step 8: Cancel like units of measurement and carry over the remaining unit of measurement to the answer.

Example: Convert 12 teaspoons to cups.

If you do not know the direct conversion from teaspoons to cups, you can go one step at a time and convert what you know.

step 1: Convert teaspoons to tablespoons.

$$\frac{12 \; \cancel{tsp}}{1} \times \frac{1 \; tbsp}{3 \; \cancel{tsp}} = \frac{12}{3} = 4 \; tbsp$$

step 2: Convert tablespoons to cups.

$$\frac{12 \; \cancel{tsp}}{1} \times \frac{1 \; tbsp}{3 \; \cancel{tsp}} = \frac{12}{3} = 4 \; tbsp$$

$$\frac{4 \; \cancel{tbsp}}{1} \times \frac{1 \; cup}{16 \; \cancel{tbsp}} = \frac{4}{16} = .25 \; cup \; or \; \frac{1}{4} \; cup$$

The calculations indicate that 12 teaspoons are equal to 1/4 cup.

If you know there are 48 teaspoons in a cup, the conversion can be done more directly:

$$\frac{12 \; \cancel{tsp}}{1} \times \frac{1 \; cup}{48 \; \cancel{tsp}} = \frac{12}{48} = .25 \; cup \; or \; \frac{1}{4} \; cup$$

The conversion may be done either way, and the results will be the same.

Conclusion

SOME PEOPLE FIND the bridge method cumbersome and get frustrated with it. However, once it is mastered, any conversion calculation can be done with confidence. Eventually you will be able to solve problems dealing with conversions without the formality of writing down the steps. It is similar to what happens when you have made a recipe many times; eventually you no longer have to look at that recipe for direction because you have memorized it.

Example: Convert 66 ounces to pounds.

Bridge Method

$$\frac{66 \; \cancel{oz}}{1} \times \frac{1 \; lb}{16 \; \cancel{oz}} = \frac{66}{16} = 4.125 \; lbs \; or \; 4\frac{1}{8} \; lbs$$

A Shortcut

Some people are able to see the 66 ounces and know to divide by 16:

$$\frac{66}{16} = 4.125 \text{ lbs or } 4\frac{1}{8} \text{ lbs}$$

Be careful doing calculations using the shortcut because it is very easy to perform the wrong operations and end up with the wrong answer. For instance, many times students will *multiply* 66 by 16 and end up with 1,056 lbs—though if you take the time to determine if the answer is reasonable, as suggested in Chapter 1, you will see that this cannot be right.

Chapter in Review

Convert the following using the bridge method.

1. 23# = _____ oz

2. 5 gallons = _____ qt

3. 29 pints = _____ cups

4. 354 tsp = _____ cups

5. 78 cups = _____ quarts

6. 88 oz = _____ #

7. $2\frac{1}{2}$ cups = _____ tbsp

8. 35 tbsp = _____ cups

9. 14 tsp = _____ tbsp

10. 24 tsp = _____ cups

11. $2\frac{3}{4}$ pecks = _____ quarts

12. .625 bushels = _____ gallons

13. 55 tsp = _____ cups

14. 48 cups = _____ quarts

15. $3\frac{1}{2}$ quarts = _____ pints

16. 3.595# = _____ oz

17. 7 pints = _____ tbsp

18. 3.5 bushels = _____ pints

19. 10 quarts = _____ gallons

20. $6\frac{1}{4}$ cups = _____ tsp

21. 4 pints = _____ quarts

22. $1\frac{3}{4}$ cups = _____ tsp

23. 18 tsp = _____ cups

24. $\frac{3}{4}$ qt = _____ gallon

25. 26 tbsp = _____ cups

26. 125 tbsp = _____ qt

27. 2 pecks = _____ gal

28. 10 gallons = _____ bushel

29. 8.5 qt = _____ gallons

30. $\frac{1}{8}$ pint = _____ tbsp

31. $\frac{1}{4}$ cups = _____ tsp

32. 15 oz = _____ #

33. 210 cups = _____ gallons

34. $14\frac{3}{4}$ pecks = _____ bushels

35. 11 tbsp = _____ tsp

36. $\frac{1}{10}$ oz = _____ #

37. $\frac{1}{5}$ peck = _____ cups

38. $\frac{1}{4}$ cup = _____ tbsp

39. .25# = _____ oz

40. 17 qt = _____ pecks

41. 9 tbsp = _____ tsp

42. $\frac{1}{10}$ cup = _____ tbsp

goals

- Convert mixed units of measure to a single unit

- Convert a single unit of measure to mixed units of measure

Converting to and from Mixed Measures within Weight or Volume

You have a recipe that calls for 3 pounds 4 ounces of flour. Flour is purchased by the pound, so this quantity must be converted to 3.25 pounds so that you may place the order. Converting to and from mixed measures will help in preparing, costing, and ordering ingredients for a recipe.

Converting single units of measure to mixed units of measure will help in the physical measuring of ingredients by saving time and reducing the chance for error. Imagine you had to increase the yield of a recipe for hot and spicy eggplant to meet your needs, and now it calls for 18 tablespoons of chopped scallions. In this instance it is more reasonable to convert the 18 tablespoons to a mixed unit of measure, as it is more practical to measure 1 cup and 2 tablespoons of chopped scallions than 18 tablespoons.

The Bridge Method

YOU HAVE A RECIPE that calls for 3 lbs 4 oz of flour. You purchase flour by the pound and therefore need to convert this quantity so that it is all in pounds. In examining this mixed measure, you see that the 3 lbs is already in pounds, but the 4 oz must be converted to pounds using the bridge method.

$$4 \text{ oz} = \frac{4 \cancel{oz}}{1} \times \frac{1 \text{ lb}}{16 \cancel{oz}} = \frac{4}{16} = .25 \text{ lbs} + 3 \text{ lbs} = 3.25 \text{ lbs}$$

You have converted the yield of a recipe, and it now calls for 18 tbsp of chopped scallions. To save time and reduce the chance for error, you need to convert this to a larger unit of measure. Using the bridge method, the problem can be set up as follows:

$$\frac{18 \cancel{tbsp}}{1} \times \frac{1 \text{ cup}}{16 \cancel{tbsp}} = \frac{18}{16} = 1.125 \text{ cups}$$

It wouldn't be reasonable to ask someone to measure 1.125 cups. However, there are 16 tablespoons in 1 cup, and 16 divides evenly into 18 one time with 2 left over. Therefore, 1.125 cups is equivalent to 1 cup plus 2 tablespoons.

As another example, problem 25 from the end of Chapter 3 reads as follows:

26 tbsp = _____ cups

You should have gotten 1.625 cups as an answer. If you need to measure this amount, it would be more helpful to convert the .625 to an easily measurable quantity.

The first step is to convert tablespoons to cups:

$$\frac{26 \cancel{tbsp}}{1} \times \frac{1 \text{ cup}}{16 \cancel{tbsp}} = \frac{26}{16} = 1.625 \text{ cups}$$

Next, convert the .625 cups back to tablespoons:

$$\frac{.625 \cancel{cups}}{1} \times \frac{16 \text{ tbsp}}{1 \cancel{cup}} = 10 \text{ tbsp}$$

Thus 1.625 cups is equal to 1 cup plus 10 tablespoons. However, measuring out 10 tablespoons could take a lot of time and increases the possibility of error. Is there a better way to measure 10 tablespoons? Consider that 8 tablespoons is equal to 1/2 cup. Subtract 8 tablespoons from 10 tablespoons and there are 2 tablespoons remaining. So an easy way to write 1.625 cups is 1 1/2 cups plus 2 tablespoons.

With this type of conversion, there will be more than one correct answer. For instance, a recipe may call for 3# 4 oz, 3.25 lbs, or 52 ounces of sugar; all of these amounts are the same, only expressed in different units. Each unit of measure may be best suited for one particular application:

- The 3# 4 oz. measure of sugar may be preferred for weighing out mise en place (the preparation and assembly of ingredients and equipment needed for a particular dish or service) instead of 3.25# if you are not working with a digital scale.
- The pound measure may be necessary for ordering, as many items like sugar are sold by the pound.
- The ounce measurement may be the easiest to use for costing if the price per ounce is known. An example of this would be most spices.

Conclusion

CONVERTING UNITS OF MEASURE to more reasonable quantities is an important skill that all professional chefs should be proficient at. Much time and money may be wasted when poor measurement quantities are used. Knowing the weight and volume equivalents is critical for the successful application of this math.

Chapter in Review

Convert each given measurement to the unit stated directly above. Show all work.

1. Represent as ounces:

   A. 4# 11 oz

   B. 6.25#

2. Represent as pounds:

   A. 5# 6 oz

   B. 115 oz

3. Represent as quarts:

   A. 16 qt 3 tbsp

   B. 1 quart 2 pints

4. Represent as cups:

   A. 2 cups 18 tbsp

   B. 1 gallon 2 pints

5. Represent as tablespoons:

   A. 3 tbsp 12 tsp

   B. $\frac{1}{4}$ cups 6 tsp

6. Represent as gallons:

   A. 6 gallons 2 cups

   B. 2 pecks 1 quart

7. Represent as pounds:

A. 20# 9 oz

B. 3# 3 oz

C. 110# 14 oz

D. 12# 1 oz

8. Represent as quarts:

A. 4 qt 4 cups

B. $2\frac{1}{2}$ qt 2 pt

C. $8\frac{3}{4}$ qt $5\frac{1}{2}$ cups

D. 12 qt 12 tablespoon

9. Represent as pints:

A. 4 pints 3 quarts

B. 2 pints 1 gallon

C. $\frac{3}{4}$ pint 2 cups

D. $12\frac{1}{2}$ cups $12\frac{1}{2}$ tbsp

10. Represent as ounces:

A. 28#

B. .375#

C. 2# 9 oz

D. 9.3333#

11. Represent as cups:

A. 1 quart 4 pints

B. 15 teaspoons

C. 3 gal 2 qt

D. 48 tablespoons

12. Represent as gallons:

A. 8 qt 10 pints

B. 3 pt 108 tbsp

C. 7 gal 120 quarts

D. 52 cups

13. Represent as tablespoons:

A. $\frac{3}{4}$ cup

B. $\frac{1}{8}$ pint

C. 18 teaspoons

D. .0625 cups

14. Represent as teaspoons:

A. $\frac{1}{14}$ cup

B. .0123 pint

C. 1.5 tablespoons

D. .125 cups

15. You receive a case of tomato juice. Each case contains four 1-gallon containers of juice. If you serve fifteen 4-fluid ounce portions of the juice, what percent of the juice will be left over?

16. You are preparing tarts. Each tart shell consists of 12 ounces of flour. If you prepare 40 tarts, how many pounds of flour do you need?

17. A recipe calls for 1/3 cup of milk. You wish to make half of the recipe. How many tablespoons of milk should you use? What would be the best way to measure the amount needed?

18. You have a case of green beans, which weighs 25 pounds. You clean and trim the beans, and 22 pounds 6 ounces of the beans remain. What percent of the original 25 pounds of beans are clean?

19. After adjusting a recipe for soup, you have 147 cups of water. What would be a better way of expressing this amount?

20. A bag of flour has 42 pounds 8 ounces remaining in it. You estimate that you have used 15 percent of the flour. How many pounds of flour did the bag originally hold?

21. You have 32 teaspoons. What percent of a cup does this represent?

22. Forty ounces of water are equivalent to _____ quarts.

23. You are serving 3-ounce portions of fruit salad. How many full portions can be obtained from 6 pounds 10 ounces of fruit salad?

24. Three tablespoons are equivalent to what percent of a pint?

25. Three pecks are equivalent to _____ bushels.

26. You need to increase a recipe by 40 percent. The original recipe calls for 1 1/2 pints of cream. How many pints of cream should you use to make the new recipe?

goals

- Identify when to use the Approximate Volume to Weight chart without error.

- Convert unit measures from weight to volume and volume to weight.

Advanced Conversions with Units of Measure between Weight and Volume

You have been hired to cater a party and are calculating the cost of the food. One of the dishes you will be preparing is green beans with walnuts. The recipe calls for 1 1/2 cups of walnuts. In order to know the amount to charge for the dish, you need to calculate the cost of each ingredient. You look up walnuts on the invoice from the purveyor and find that they are sold by the pound, not by the cup. Pounds are a unit of weight, while cups are a unit of volume. To figure out the cost, you need to convert the cups into pounds.

For this same party you made carrot cake. One of the guests asked for the recipe, which calls for 3 3/4 pounds of all-purpose flour. Most people do not have a kitchen scale and are not familiar with weighing ingredients for baking or cooking. You want to convert the weight unit into a volume unit the guest will be more familiar with.

In this chapter you will discover how to handle these types of situations, using the Approximate Volume to Weight chart.

Approximate Equivalent of Food Measures

MOST OF THE TIME, a food that is measured by volume (teaspoons, tablespoons, cups, pints, or quarts) does not weigh the number of ounces that would be contained in that measure if given in fluid ounces. A fluid ounce is a measure that is based on the amount of space filled by 1 ounce of water. You cannot assume that any other substance has the same density as water and will therefore weigh the same as water or water-like liquids (see Figure 5.1).

If you fill a measuring cup with honey and place it on a scale, it will not weigh 8 ounces (as water would), but will weigh 12 ounces. If something other than water is being measured by volume, do not make the common mistake of assuming that "a pint is a pound the world round." If you are dealing with something other than water, you have two choices: weigh the measured volume of the ingredient, or use the Approximate Volume to Weight chart provided in this chapter to calculate the conversion. While it may be more convenient to use a chart to make the calculations, be aware that any information in this chart or any chart such as this is an approximation, and if accuracy is important, the measurement should be weighed.

FIGURE 5.1. **Eight ounces by weight of oregano is a much larger quantity than 8 fluid ounces. Weight and volume measurements should never be confused.**

Introduction to the Approximate Volume to Weight Chart

THE FOLLOWING CHART provides information for converting between volume and weight measures. The first column lists the item. The second column gives a volume measure: tablespoon (T), cup (C), or each. The last column gives the approximate weight, in ounces, of the given volume measure for that particular item.

Let's take a look at how the information in the chart is laid out:

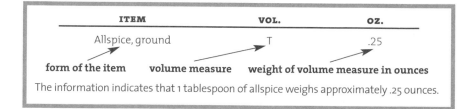

ITEM	VOL.	OZ.
Allspice, ground	T	.25

form of the item   volume measure   weight of volume measure in ounces

The information indicates that 1 tablespoon of allspice weighs approximately .25 ounces.

APPROXIMATE VOLUMES TO WEIGHTS

ITEM	VOL.	OZ.	ITEM	VOL.	OZ.
Allspice, ground	T	1/4	Bread crumbs, soft	C	2
Almonds, blanched	C	5 1/3	Brussels sprouts *	C	4
Apples, peeled, 1/2" cubes	C	3 1/3	Butter	C	8
Applesauce, canned	C	8	Cabbage, shredded †	C	4
Apples, pie, canned	C	6	Cake crumbs, soft	C	2 3/4
Apricots, drained	C	5 1/3	Carrots, raw or cooked, diced	C	5 1/3
Apricots, cooked	C	3 1/3	Celery, diced †	C	4
Apricots, halves	C	8	Celery seed	T	1/4
Apricots, pie, packed	C	9	Cheese, cottage or cream	C	8
Asparagus, cut, canned	C	6 1/2	Cheese, grated	C	4
Baking powder	T	1/2	Cherries, glacéed	C	6 1/2
Baking powder	C	8	Chicken, cooked, cubed	C	5 1/3
Bananas, diced	C	6 1/2	Chili powder	T	1/4
Barley	C	8	Chili sauce	C	11 1/4
Beans, baked	C	8	Chocolate, grated	C	4 1/2
Beans, lima, dried	C	6 1/2	Chocolate, melted	C	8
Beans, lima, cooked	C	8	Cinnamon, ground	T	1/4
Beans, kidney	C	6	Citron, dried, chopped	C	6 1/2
Beans, kidney, cooked	C	6 3/4	Cloves, ground	T	1/4
Beans, navy, dried	C	6 3/4	Cloves, whole	C	3
Beans, navy, cooked	C	5 1/3	Cocoa	C	4
Beans, cut, canned, drained	C	4 1/2	Coconut, shredded	C	2 1/2
Bean sprouts	C	4	Corn, canned	C	8
Beets, cooked, diced	C	6 1/2	Corn flakes	C	1
Beets, cooked, sliced	C	6 1/2	Cornmeal *	C	5 1/3
Blueberries, fresh	C	7	Corn syrup	C	12
Blueberries, canned	C	6 1/2	Cornstarch	T	1/4
Bread crumbs, dried	C	4	Cornstarch	C	4 1/2

(continued)

*As-purchased quantity †Edible portion quantity

ITEM	VOL.	OZ.	ITEM	VOL.	OZ.
Cracker crumbs	C	3	Ham, cooked, diced	C	5 1/3
Cranberries, raw	C	4	Honey	C	12
Cranberry sauce	C	8	Horseradish	T	1/2
Cream of tartar	T	1/3	Jam	C	12
Cream of wheat	C	6	Jelly	C	10 2/3
Cream, whipping	C	8	Lard	C	8
Cream, whipped	C	4	Lettuce, shredded	C	2 1/4
Cucumbers, diced	C	5 1/3	Margarine	C	8
Currants, dried	C	5 1/3	Marshmallows, large	80 ea	16
Curry powder	T	1/4	Mayonnaise	C	8
Dates, pitted	C	6 1/5	Meat, cooked, chopped	C	8
Eggs, dried, whites	C	3 1/4	Milk, liquid	C	8 1/2
Eggs, dried, yolks	C	2 3/4	Milk, condensed	C	10 2/3
Eggs, fresh, whites (9)	C	8	Milk, evaporated	C	9
Eggs, fresh, yolks (10)	C	8	Milk, nonfat dry	C	4
Eggs, raw, shelled (5 eggs)	C	8	Milk, nonfat dry	T	1/4
Farina, raw	C	5 1/3	Mincemeat	C	8
Figs, dried, chopped	C	6 1/2	Molasses	C	12
Flour, all-purpose	C	4	Mustard, dry, ground	C	3 1/2
Flour, bread, unsifted	C	4 1/2	Mustard, prepared	T	1/2
Flour, bread, sifted	C	4	Mustard seed	T	2/5
Flour, cake/pastry, sifted	C	3 1/3	Noodles, cooked	C	5 1/3
Flour, rye	C	2 3/4	Nutmeats	C	4 1/2
Flour, soy	C	3 1/4	Nutmeg, ground	T	1/4
Flour, whole wheat	C	4 1/4	Oil, vegetable	C	8
Gelatin, granulated	T	1/4	Onions, chopped	C	6 1/2
Gelatin, granulated	C	5 1/3	Oysters, shucked	C	8
Ginger, ground	T	1/5	Paprika	T	1/4
Ginger, ground	C	3 1/4	Parsley, coarsely chopped	C	1
Grapes, cut, seeded	C	5 3/4	Peanuts †	C	5
Grapes, whole	C	4	Peanut butter	C	9

ITEM	VOL.	OZ.	ITEM	VOL.	OZ.
Peaches, chopped	C	8	Sauerkraut	C	5 1/3
Peas, canned, drained	C	8	Sesame seed	T	1/3
Peas, dried, split	C	6 3/4	Sesame seed	C	5 3/8
Pears, canned, drain/diced	C	6 1/2	Shallots, diced	T	2/5
Pecans †	C	4 1/2	Shortening	C	7
Pepper, ground	T	1/4	Soda, baking	T	2/5
Pepper, ground	C	4	Soybeans	C	7
Peppers, green, chopped	C	5 1/3	Spinach, raw	Qt	3 1/4
Pimiento, chopped	C	6 1/2	Spinach, cooked	C	8
Pineapple, crushed	C	8	Squash, Hubbard, cooked	C	8
Poppy seed	C	5	Strawberries	C	7
Potatoes, cooked, diced/mashed	C	8	Suet, ground	C	4 1/2
Potato chips	C	1	Sugar, brown, lightly packed	C	5 1/3
Prunes, dried	C	6 1/2	Sugar, brown, solidly packed	C	8
Prunes, cooked, pitted	C	5	Sugar, granulated	C	8
Pumpkin, cooked	C	6 1/2	Sugar, powered, sifted	C	5 1/3
Raisins	C	5 1/3	Tapioca, quick-cooking	C	5 1/3
Raisins, after cooking	C	7	Tapioca, pearl	C	5 3/4
Raspberries *	C	4 3/4	Tea, loose-leaf	C	2 2/3
Rhubarb, cooked	C	6 1/2	Tea, instant	C	2
Rhubarb, raw, 1" dice	C	4	Tomatoes, canned	C	8
Rice, uncooked	C	8	Tomatoes, fresh, diced	C	7
Rice, cooked	C	8 1/2	Tuna	C	8
Rice, puffed	C	3/5	Vanilla	T	1/2
Rutabaga, cubed	C	4 3/4	Vinegar	C	8
Sage, ground	C	2	Walnuts, shelled	C	4
Salad dressing	C	8	Water	C	8
Salmon, canned	C	8	Yeast, compressed cake	each	3/5
Salt	T	2/3	Yeast, envelope	each	1/4

*As-purchased quantity   †Edible portion quantity

Solving Problems Using the Approximate Volume to Weight Chart

A RECIPE CALLS for 24 tablespoons of walnuts. To determine the cost of the recipe, the weight equivalent in pounds must be calculated. The following steps demonstrate the method for making this conversion:

1. Use the Approximate Volume to Weight chart to find the weight of walnuts. According to the chart, 1 cup of walnuts weighs 4 ounces.

2. Convert the 24 tablespoons into cups, because the chart gives the weight of 1 cup of walnuts, not 1 tablespoon. Use the bridge method to make this calculation.

$$\frac{24 \text{ tbsp}}{1} \times \frac{1 \text{ cup}}{16 \text{ tbsp}} = 1.5 \text{ cups}$$

3. Convert the cups to ounces, and the ounces to pounds.

$$\frac{1.5 \text{ cups}}{1} \times \frac{4 \text{ ounces}}{1 \text{ cup}} = \frac{6 \text{ ounces}}{1} \times \frac{1 \text{ pound}}{16 \text{ ounces}} = .375 \text{ pounds}$$

The calculations show that 24 tablespoons of walnuts are equivalent to 6 ounces or .375 pounds. The figure .375 pounds may seem to be an awkward number to work with, but it is the number necessary to find the cost of the walnuts. (Finding cost will be covered in Chapter 7, and recipe costing in Chapter 9.)

As another example, a recipe for carrot cake calls for 3 3/4 pounds of all-purpose flour. A customer requested this recipe, and as most people do not have a kitchen scale in their home, you would like to convert the 3 3/4 pounds of all-purpose flour into a cup measurement (see Figure 5.2).

1. Consult the Approximate Volume to Weight chart to find the weight of all-purpose flour. According to the chart, 1 cup of all-purpose flour weighs 4 ounces.

2. Convert the 3 3/4 pounds into ounces first, because the chart gives the weight of 1 cup of all-purpose flour in ounces, not in pounds. Use the bridge method to make this calculation.

$$\frac{3.75 \text{ pounds}}{1} \times \frac{16 \text{ ounces}}{1 \text{ pound}} = 60 \text{ ounces}$$

3. Convert the ounces to cups:

$$\frac{60 \text{ ounces}}{1} \times \frac{1 \text{ cup}}{4 \text{ ounces}} = 15 \text{ cups}$$

The calculations indicate that 60 ounces of all-purpose flour are equivalent to 15 cups.

CARROT CAKE
Ingredients measured by Weight and by Volume

MEASURED BY WEIGHT	INGREDIENT	MEASURED BY VOLUME
1/4 lb	butter	1/2 cup
1/2 lb	granulated sugar	1 1/8 cup
1/2 lb	light brown sugar	1 cup, packed
8 oz	eggs	4 each
1 lb	grated carrots	4 cups
1 oz	lemon juice	2 tbsp
1 oz	orange juice	2 tbsp
1/2 oz	lemon zest	5 tbsp
1/2 oz	orange zest	5 tbsp
15 oz	all purpose flour	3 3/4 cups
.33 oz	baking powder	1 tbsp 1tsp
.25 oz	baking soda	1 3/4 tsp
.25 oz	salt	1 tsp
.25 oz	ground cinnamon	1 tbsp
5 oz	chopped walnuts	1 1/4 cups

FIGURE 5.2. The ingredients for a carrot cake recipe are shown by weight on the left and by volume on the right. The ingredients are equivalent, but two types of measurement were used. Both groups of ingredients give the same yield.

Conclusion

CONVERTING BETWEEN VOLUME and weight is a skill that any professional chef needs to master in order to effectively manage the costs in a kitchen. Additionally, recipes that are used in a professional kitchen will need to be adjusted for the home cook or to produce a larger or smaller quantity of the recipe. When this is done, the ingredients quantity will need to be altered depending on the intended use of the recipe.

Chapter in Review

Find the answer to the following questions, using the Approximate Volume to Weight chart on page 45 if necessary.

1. A recipe calls for 5 1/3 cups of cocoa. How many pounds of cocoa do you need to use?

2. How many cups can be measured from 4 pounds of honey?

3. How many pounds of Parmesan cheese must you purchase in order to have 5 cups of grated cheese? *Hint:* Look under "Cheese, grated" for the weight/volume conversion for Parmesan cheese.

4. If a recipe calls for 2 gallons of fresh diced tomatoes, how many pounds should you use?

5. How many ounces are in 3 tablespoons of peanut butter?

6. How many tablespoons are in 1 pound of cinnamon?

7. You need 6 cups of raw cream of wheat. How many 1-pound boxes of cream of wheat would you need to buy?

8. A recipe for chocolate-coated almonds calls for 2 tablespoons of cocoa. How many ounces of cocoa should you use?

9. How many pounds of diced shallots should you use if a recipe calls for 3 1/4 cups?

10. How much would 1 teaspoon of cumin weigh if 1 cup of cumin weighs 4 ounces?

11. How many tablespoons of salt would be in a container of salt that weighs 1 pound 10 ounces?

12. You are ordering ham for a breakfast you will be serving. You will be making omelets for 85 guests. Each omelet will need 1/3 cup of cooked diced ham. What is the minimal amount of ham, in pounds, that you should order to make the omelets?

13. You have a container of chili powder that contains 1 pound 3 ounces. How many tablespoons will you be able to measure from the container?

14. You have a banquet for 2,500 people. Dessert will be tapioca pudding. Your recipe calls for 1 cup of pearl tapioca for every 4 portions. How many pounds of pearl tapioca do you need to purchase?

15. How many ounces are in a cup of cinnamon?

16. How many ounces of diced shallots are in 1 cup?

17. You are making a dozen mini strawberry pies. The recipe for one pie calls for 3/4 cup of granulated sugar. How many pounds of sugar do you need?

18. A recipe calls for 3/4 cup of dry raisins. If you are doubling the recipe, how many pounds of raisins should you use?

19. After increasing a recipe, you determine that you will need 10 cups of all-purpose flour. How many pounds of all-purpose flour do you need to use?

20. A recipe calls for 3 1/2 cups of dried lima beans. How many pounds should you add to the recipe?

21. How many cups of rice are in a 50-pound bag of rice?

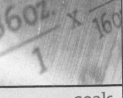

CHAPTER 6

Yield Percentage

goals

- Define the various components of a yield test
- Use the terms *as-purchased quantity (APQ)*, *edible portion quantity (EPQ)*, and *trim* correctly
- Calculate the yield percentage
- Identify the factors that might affect yield percentage
- Distinguish the times when it is appropriate to use the yield percentage chart

You are catering a party for 150 guests, and the food order must be in by noon today. One of the side dishes that you plan to serve is potatoes au gratin. You need 33 pounds 12 ounces of peeled, sliced potatoes for this recipe. Potatoes are ordered unpeeled; therefore you will need a greater amount of unpeeled potatoes to yield 33 pounds 12 ounces of peeled, sliced potatoes needed for the dish. If you purchased just 33 pounds 12 ounces of the uncleaned, unpeeled potatoes, there would not be enough to make the correct amount of potatoes au gratin for the event.

To get the desired weight of a cleaned and peeled (fabricated) product, the uncleaned and unpeeled weight of the product must be calculated. The factor used to make this calculation is called the yield percentage.

As-purchased quantity of potatoes and edible portion quantity of potatoes.

Definitions

As-Purchased Quantity (APQ)

As-purchased quantity is defined as the weight, volume, or count of the non-fabricated fruit or vegetable. In other words, it is the quantity (weight, volume, or count) of the product as it is received from the vendor. The illustration of the potato above is in as-purchased condition. A 50# bag of potatoes, before fabrication, is the as-purchased quantity (APQ).

Edible Portion Quantity (EPQ)

The edible portion quantity is defined as the weight volume or count of the fabricated fruit or vegetable. In other words it is the quantity (weight, volume, or count) of the product after it has been cleaned, peeled, or prepared (fabricated) and is ready for use. The word *edible* in this term indicated the condition of the product as ready for use in preparing a dish. If you were to peel a 50# bag of potatoes, you would have a pile of cleaned potatoes ready to be used in a dish; this is the edibleportion quantity (EPQ). The weight of these peeled potatoes would be approximately 42.5 pounds.

> **Chef's Note**
>
> Most professional recipes list ingredients and quantities in edible portion form. However, it is important to be aware and read through the recipe directions to determine the form in which the ingredients are listed.

Trim

Trim is defined as the weight or volume of the waste. Trim, mathematically speaking, is the difference between APQ and EPQ:

$$APQ - EPQ = Trim$$

A 50-pound bag of potatoes yields approximately 42.5 pounds of cleaned, peeled potatoes, leaving approximately 7.5 pounds of trim (in this case, peels).

$$50 \text{ lbs} - 42.5 \text{ lbs} = 7.5 \text{ lbs}$$

Not all trim is loss. Many say that if the trim is usable, then it is not a loss. For instance, the potato peels may be used in a vegetable stock (though the value of those potato skins is so small it would not be worth allocating their cost to the soup in a cost determination—see Chapter 9). Using the trim instead of throwing it away will make a kitchen run more cost-effectively. Whether and how the potato skins are used determines if the trim is loss.

Yield Percentage

YIELD PERCENTAGE is the percentage of the as-purchased quantity that is edible (see Figure 6.2).

There are three major applications for yield percentage:

1. Computing the minimum amount to order

2. Recipe costing

3. Determining the maximum number of servings that a purchased amount will yield

FIGURE 6.2. Melon, in this case cantaloupe, has a yield percentage of 50 percent, which means that the edible portion quantity is one-half of the total as-purchased quantity.

The Math of Calculating Yield Percentage

Yield Percentage Formula

$$\text{Yield Percentage} = \frac{\text{Edible Portion Quantity}}{\text{As-Purchased Quantity}} \times 100$$

The EPQ, APQ, and Yield Percentage Triangle

The following triangle is a tool used to find the yield percentage, as-purchased quantity, and edible portion quantity. It is identical to the Percentage Triangle introduced in Chapter 1, although the application differs.

Part = Edible Portion Quantity
Whole = As-Purchased Quantity
Percent = Yield Percentage

EPQ/APQ/Y% (Yield Percentage) Triangle Directions

1. Determine what you are looking for: EPQ, APQ, or yield percentage.

2. *To find the edible portion quantity (EPQ):*

   Cover the EPQ for edible portion quantity.

   APQ and Y% are side by side. This directs you to multiply the APQ by the yield percentage. (Remember to change the percentage to a decimal by dividing by 100.)

   To find the as-purchased quantity (APQ):

   Cover the APQ for as-purchased quantity.

   EPQ is over Y%. This directs you to divide the EPQ by the yield percentage. (Remember to change the percentage to a decimal by dividing by 100.)

   To find the yield percentage:

   Cover the Y% for yield percentage.

   EPQ is over APQ. This directs you to divide the EPQ by the APQ and multiply the answer by 100 to convert it to the yield percentage.

Steps for Calculating the Yield Percentage

There are three steps necessary to calculate the yield percentage:

1. To calculate the yield percentage for the potatoes, you must first identify the EPQ and the APQ.

2. Determine if the units are the same before calculating the yield percentage. Use the bridge method (Chapter 3) if necessary.

3. Substitute the weights of the EPQ and APQ into the formula and solve.

Example: Fifty pounds of potatoes have been purchased. If the potatoes are weighed after cleaning and peeling, there will be approximately 42.5 pounds of cleaned potatoes and 7.5 pounds of trim (loss).

1. Identify the EPQ and the APQ.

   APQ = 50 pounds (whole potatoes)
   EPQ = 42.5 pounds (cleaned and peeled potatoes)

2. Determine if the units are the same before calculating the yield percentage. Use the bridge method (Chapter 3) if necessary. In this problem, both the EPQ and the APQ are in pounds. We can continue.

3. Substitute the weights of the EPQ and APQ into the formula and solve.

$$\text{Yield Percentage} = \frac{\text{EPQ}}{\text{APQ}} = \frac{42.5 \text{ lbs}}{50 \text{ lbs}} = .85 \times 100 = 85\%$$

The calculations indicate that the yield percentage for potatoes is 85 percent.

It is important to recognize that the 50 pounds of potatoes or the as-purchased quantity represents 100 percent. After cleaning and peeling the potatoes there will be the cleaned, peeled potatoes and the peels (trim) The 42.5 pounds of cleaned potatoes (the edible portion quantity) represents 85 percent of the as-purchased quantity; this is the yield percentage. The percent that is not usable in this application is the trim loss percentage, in this case 15 percent (100% − 85% = 15%). The yield percentage and the trim loss percentage add up to 100 percent and the EPQ and trim add up to the APQ. See the diagram below.

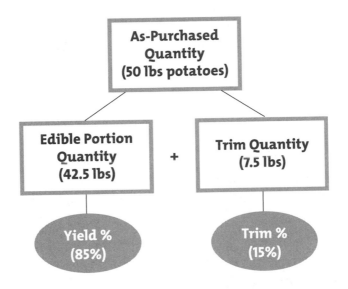

Example: You purchase a 5-pound bag of lemons and juice them. When you finish, you have 36 ounces of lemon juice. What is the yield percentage for lemon juice?

1. Identify the EPQ and the APQ.

APQ = 5 pounds (whole lemons)
EPQ = 36.5 ounces (lemon juice)

2. Determine if the units are the same before calculating the yield percentage. Use the bridge method (Chapter 3) if necessary. In this case, the units are not the same. Let's convert the 36.5 ounces to pounds.

$$\frac{36.5 \cancel{oz}}{1} \times \frac{1 \text{ lb.}}{16 \cancel{oz}} = \frac{36.5}{16} = 2.28125 \text{ pounds of lemon juice}$$

Now that both values are in pounds, proceed. Keep in mind that the APQ could have been converted so that both values were in ounces. Either approach would have the same end result.

3. Substitute the EPQ and APQ values into the formula and solve.

$$\text{Yield Percentage} = \frac{EPQ}{APQ} = \frac{2.28125 \text{ lbs}}{5 \text{ lbs}} = .456 \times 100 = 45.6\%$$

After rounding, it is safe to say that 45 percent of the weight of the lemons purchased will be juice.

ROUNDING

Yield percentage is a mathematical prediction of the percentage of a food that is usable. In this case, we are predicting that 45.6 percent of the lemons, by weight, will be juice when squeezed. We could leave that number as is (45.6 percent) or we could round it. Rules of mathematics say to round such a figure up; however, rounding it up to 46 percent would allot a greater yield to the lemons. As a rule, yield percentages should be rounded down to the next lower whole number to ensure that enough product is ordered to provide the necessary yield.

Using the Approximate Yield of Fruits and Vegetables Chart

YIELD PERCENTAGE is a very useful tool. Often there will not be sufficient time to do an actual yield test. The following chart is designed to provide yield information for a sampling of fruits and vegetables. There are more exhaustive sources available; however, the problems that appear in this textbook use the information from the yield percentage chart contained in this chapter.

The chart provides the yield percentages of the listed fruits and vegetables and information regarding the as-purchased weight of certain fruits and vegetables. For example, the listing for celery gives the average weight of a bunch of celery (2 pounds). Another example is coconut—the average weight of a coconut is 26 ounces. This information will become very useful in later chapters.

APPROXIMATE YIELDS OF FRUITS AND VEGETABLES

APPROX. WGT/EA	ITEM	YIELD %	APPROX. WGT/EA	ITEM	YIELD %
2# ea	Anise	75		Collards	77
	Apples	76	.58# ea	Cucumbers	95
	Apricots	94	1.25# ea	Eggplant	81
	Artichokes	48		Endive, chicory, escarole	74
	Asparagus	56		Figs	82
	Avocado	75		Fruit for juice*	
.44# ea	Bananas	68	16 oz	Grapefruit	45*
	Beans, green/ wax	88	3.5 oz	Lemon	45*
	Beans, lima, in shell	40	2.2 oz	Lime	35*
			6.6 oz	Oranges, Fla.	50*
	Beets, no tops	76	.125# ea	Garlic bulb (10–12 cloves)	87
	Beets, with tops	49		Grapefruit sections	47
	Beet greens	56			
	Blackberries	92		Grapes, seedless	94
	Blueberries	92		Kale	74
1.5# bu	Broccoli	61		Kohlrabi	55
	Brussels sprouts	74	.75# bu	Leeks	52
2.5# ea	Cabbage, green	79	2.25# head	Lettuce, iceberg	74
	Cantaloupe, no rind	50		Lettuce, leaf	67
	Carrots, no tops	82		Melons:	
	Carrots, with tops	60		Cantaloupe	50
2# head	Cauliflower	45		Casaba	50
2# bu	Celery	75		Cranshaw	50
	Celery root (celeriac)	75		Honeydew, no rind	60
	Chard	77		Watermelon, flesh	46
26 oz ea	Coconut	53		Mushrooms	97
				Mustard greens	68

(continued)

*the yield percentages of producing juice.

APPROXIMATE YIELDS OF FRUITS AND VEGETABLES (CON'T)

APPROX. WGT/EA	ITEM	YIELD %	APPROX. WGT/EA	ITEM	YIELD %
	Nectarines	86		Potatoes, chef	85
	Okra	78		Potatoes, sweet	80
.33# bu	Onions, green (10–12)	60		Radishes, with tops	63
	Onions, large	89		Radishes, no tops	85
	Orange sections	70		Raspberries	97
.33# bu	Parsley	76		Rhubarb, no leaves	86
	Parsnips	85	3# ea	Rutabagas	85
	Peaches	76		Salsify	63
	Pears	78	.03# ea	Shallots	89
	Peas, green, in the shell	38		Spinach	74
.33# ea	Peppers, green	82		Squash:	
.19# ea	Peppers, fryers	85	.83# ea	Acorn	78
	Persimmons	82	1.8# ea	Butternut	52
4# ea	Pineapple	52		Hubbard	66
	Plums, pitted	85	.36# ea	Yellow	95
	Pomegranates	54	.58# ea	Zucchini	95
	Potatoes, red	81		Strawberries	87

Factors that Affect Yield Percentage

THE APPROXIMATE YIELDS OF FRUITS AND VEGETABLES chart gives approximate yield percentages for a variety of fruits and vegetables. However, certain conditions may affect the yield percentage:

- An employee's skill in cleaning the product will have an enormous effect on the yield percentage. Some employees will clean a product using a heavy hand, resulting in more trim, whereas other employees will not create as much waste when cleaning the same product.
- The size of the product will also have an effect on the yield percentage. Cleaning small carrots will create more waste and a lower yield percentage than larger carrots cleaned in the same way because there is more surface area per unit of weight for the smaller carrots.
- The condition of the fruit or vegetable will have an effect on the yield percentage. If the product is not used while it is fresh and in its best condition, the yield percentage will be lower.

The Approximate Yields of Fruits and Vegetables chart gives the yields for fruits and vegetables in their best condition with a highly skilled individual fabricating it. Remember, these yields are approximate; if an exact yield percentage is needed for a particular situation, an actual yield test should be done. To do this, clean a sample of the product and calculate the exact yield percentage using the following steps.

Steps for an Actual Yield Test

Carrots are used in the following example, but the same procedure should be followed for all fruits and vegetables.

1. Purchase carrots.
2. Weigh the carrots (APQ).
3. Clean the carrots (peel them and trim the ends).
4. Weigh the clean carrots (EPQ).
5. Using the APQ and EPQ weights, calculate the yield percentage using the formula discussed in the beginning of the chapter.

The butcher's yield test is very similar to the yield test for fruits and vegetables.

The main difference is that the trim created during the fabrication of meat and poultry has value, whereas the trim created when you fabricate fruits and vegetables generally does not. There are several definitions and calculations for the butcher's yield test that are slightly different:

As-purchased weight: For meat and poultry, the APQ is the weight of the meat or poultry item as it is delivered from the purveyor.

Trim. The trim of meat and poultry has three components:

Fat: the weight of the fat removed during fabrication

Bones: the weight of the bones removed during fabrication

Usable trim: the weight of the trim that can be used in other preparations (ground beef, cubed beef for stew, chicken wings, etc.)

Conclusion

THE CONCEPT OF THE YIELD percentage is very important when determining how much of a product to purchase or use for a recipe. You can imagine that it would be awful to place an order for a quantity of product that is listed in the recipe and then discover that you are short because yield percentage was not taken into account! Many chefs guess at the EPQ and APQ of ingredients that they are using. Sometimes they are right, however, sometimes they are WRONG. Now you have the "tools" to be correct all the time. The only thing you must be aware of is that the fabrication skills of the people trimming the products you are using must be closely monitored.

New fabricated weight: The new fabricated weight is the as-purchased weight minus the total trim weight.

Butcher's Yield Percentage = New Fabricated Weight\As-Purchased Weight × 100

Example: You purchase rib meat that weighs 36.9 pounds. The fat weighs 8 pounds, the bones weigh 7.3 pounds, and the usable trim weighs 8.7 pounds. To calculate the butcher's yield percentage, you must first calculate the new fabricated weight:

1. Add up the weight of the trim.

    8 pounds + 7.3 pounds + 8.7 pounds = 24 pounds

2. Subtract the trim weight from the as-purchased weight to find the new fabricated weight.

    36.9 pounds − 24 pounds = 12.9 pounds

3. To find the butcher's yield, substitute the as-purchased weight and the new fabricated weight:

$$\text{Butcher's Yield Percentage} = \frac{\text{New Fabricated Weight}}{\text{As-Purchased Weight}} \times 100$$

$$= \frac{12.9\#}{36.9\#} \times 100 = .349 \times 100 = 34.9\%$$

Chapter in Review

1. What are some fruits and vegetables with a very low yield percentage?

2. What are some fruits and vegetables with a very high yield percentage?

3. Chef Linda bought 3 bunches of basil for a recipe for a brunch she is catering. Each bunch weighs 2.5 ounces, and 4.2 ounces of usable basil are yielded from all the cleaned bunches together. What is the yield percentage?

4. You purchased 25 pounds of sweet potatoes. After cleaning the potatoes, there are 6.25 pounds of peels. What is the yield percentage?

5. You purchase 6 heads of Bibb lettuce. Each head weighs 6 ounces. After cleaning the lettuce, you have 1.8 pounds of trimmed lettuce. What is the yield percentage?

6. You purchase 25 bananas. Each banana weighs approximately .44 pounds. After peeling and trimming the fruit, you have 7.1875 pounds of cleaned bananas. What is the yield percentage?

7. You purchase a case of beets that weighs 40 pounds. After cleaning the beets, you have 13 pounds 9.6 ounces of trim. What is the yield percentage?

8. Chef Julia is serving a green bean salad with feta cheese, tomatoes, and olives. She is serving 5-ounce portions to each of the 175 guests. She will need 43.75 pounds of cleaned green beans. She orders 50 pounds of green beans. What is the yield percentage?

9. You have 10 pounds of anise. After cleaning it, you have 7.5 pounds of trimmed anise. What is the yield percentage?

10. You have 25 pounds of leaf lettuce. After cleaning the lettuce, you have 8 pounds 4 ounces of outer leaves and cores. What is the yield percentage?

11. The trim-loss percentage for kohlrabi is 45 percent. What is the yield percentage?

12. You purchase 10.375 pounds of apples in order to have enough apples to make four pies. Each pie is to contain 2 pounds 1 ounce of cleaned apples. What is the yield percentage for the apples?

13. You have 6 cabbages, each weighing 2.25 pounds. If after cleaning the cabbages you are left with 170 ounces of usable cabbage, what is the yield percentage?

14. You have 9 red peppers, each weighing 5 1/3 ounces. The trim weighs 17 percent of the purchased amount, and the edibleportion quantity is 2 1/2 pounds. What is the yield percentage?

15. Explain which fruit would have a higher yield percentage when used to make fruit salad—raspberries or bananas.

16. Define yield percentage in words. How would a chef use yield percentage?

17. Using the information in this chapter, predict how many pounds of potatoes you need in order to make the potatoes au gratin discussed on page 77.

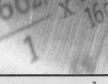

Finding Cost

goals

- Apply the cost-per-unit formula
- Solve for the total cost
- Apply the definition of cost as used by the foodservice industry

You are catering a wedding brunch for 230 guests. You predict that each guest will have approximately 2 cups of coffee. A pound of coffee will make 50 cups. The bride has requested a special blend of coffee, Kenya AA, a high-quality coffee from Africa. This coffee can be purchased for $7.95 a pound. You need to estimate the cost of the coffee for this brunch in order to determine how much to charge.

Finding cost is one of the most important parts in budgeting and predicting. Most food items purchased from suppliers are packed and priced using wholesale bulk sizes, such as crates, cases, bags, and cartons. In kitchen production, the quantity in the package may be used for several different menu items. In order to allocate the proper prices to the recipe being prepared, it is necessary to convert the price of the purchase package into unit prices, which are expressed by the price per pound, each, dozen, quart, and so on, depending on how the product is used in the recipe.

An example might be that you have just received a case of canned Italian plum tomatoes. The purchase price was $18.78, and there are six cans in a case. From this information, you can find the price per can (per item). With the two values, price per can and the amount needed for the recipe, the cost for plum tomatoes in the recipe can be calculated.

Determining Cost per Unit

THE PRICE PAID for goods is the as-purchased cost. Products are purchased in many units, such as cases, pounds, bushels, containers, ounces, grams, kilograms, liters, gallons, and dozens. It will be necessary to determine the cost per unit (per smaller unit contained in the larger unit) to determine the cost of an ingredient in a particular recipe or dish (see Figure 7.1).

To find the cost of one unit in a pack with many units, always divide the as-purchased cost (total cost) of the pack by the number of units in the pack.

$$\text{Cost per Unit} = \frac{\text{As-Purchased Cost}}{\text{Number of Units}}$$

> ## Rounding
>
> Here is another example of rounding that goes against the regular rules for rounding. For $.992, the regular rounding rules would have you round down to $.99. However, in costing, it is better to always round any partial cent up to the next higher cent. If you round down, you will be underestimating cost. So $.992 would round to $1.00.

The word *per* in this formula indicates that the cost for one unit is being calculated. The unit could be one of many things: 1 peach, 1 ounce, 1 pound, 1 package, or 1 can. When using the formula, remember that the amount of money always goes on top and the number of units goes on the bottom of the formula.

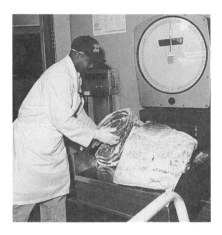

FIGURE 7.1. **The receiving area of any foodservice establishment handles goods in a wide variety of units, many of which will need to be converted for use in costing.**

This formula is often used in everyday life. For example, it is used while shopping in the supermarket, to find the best price on almost any item. For example, the cost per unit of two brands of rice can be compared to see which is the lower. If Brand A can be purchased in 1-pound boxes for $1.89 but Brand B may be purchased in a 5-pound bag for $4.96, which is cheaper? To compare these two items, the prices must be for the same unit. In other words, in this example, you need to find the price for 1 pound of rice in each package. This is the calculation that would have to be done to make the comparison:

$$\text{Cost per Unit} = \frac{\text{As-Purchased Cost}}{\text{Number of Units}} = \frac{\$4.96}{5 \text{ pounds}} = \$.992 \text{ per pound}$$

This calculation indicates that one pound of Brand B would cost $1.00. That is less than the $1.89 for 1 pound of Brand A rice. Although the total cost of the rice is $4.96, the price per pound is less.

Total Cost

WHEN CALCULATING TOTAL COST in the foodservice industry, it is important to remember that cost is based on how much of a product is used for a particular recipe, not on what is purchased. The as-purchase information is used to determine the cost per unit of the amount that is used in a particular recipe. If you are using 4 pounds of flour to make a wedding cake, but the flour was purchased in a 25-pound bag, you would want to allocate only the cost of 4 pounds of flour to the wedding cake, not the cost of 25 pounds. The cost of the remaining flour will be allocated to the other products made with the remaining 21 pounds.

Rounding

When calculating as-purchased cost, it is best not to round the number of units and the cost per unit. Rounding to the next higher cent should take place after the calculations are finished and the value for the as-purchased cost has been determined. Rounding in each step of the calculation may cause the answer to be significantly higher.

Calculating As-Purchased Cost

After the cost per unit has been calculated, the total cost formula may have to be applied to determine how much an ingredient in a particular recipe is costing you.

As-Purchased cost may be calculated using the following formula:

As-Purchased Cost = Number of Units × Cost per Unit

Must be the same unit!

Steps for Calculating As-Purchased Cost

Step 1: Read the problem to determine the quantity you are costing.

Step 2: Identify the given as-purchased cost information.

Step 3: Select the unit to be used for both the as-purchased cost and the quantity.

Step 4: Perform the calculations necessary to convert the as-purchased cost and/or the quantity to the unit chosen in step 3.

Step 5: Substitute these numbers into the as-purchased cost formula and multiply to find the as-purchased cost.

Step 6: Round any partial pennies up to the next higher cent.

Step 7: Check the answer to make sure it is reasonable.

Example: You are catering a wedding brunch for 230 guests. You are predicting that each guest will have approximately 2 cups of coffee. A pound of coffee costs $7.95 and makes 50 cups. What is the as-purchased cost of coffee for this brunch?

Step 1: Read the problem and determine the quantity you are costing.

We are costing 2 cups of coffee for 230 guests

230 × 2 cups = 460 cups total

Step 2: Identify the given as-purchased cost information.

The coffee costs $7.95 per pound.

Step 3: Select the unit to be used for both the as-purchased cost and the quantity.
Coffee is purchased by the pound, and 1 pound of coffee makes 50 cups.

It makes sense to choose pounds as the unit to use to solve this problem.

Step 4: Perform the calculations necessary to convert the as-purchased cost and/or the quantity to the unit chosen in step 3.

The coffee price is already given per pound.

The 460 cups can be converted to pounds using the given information (1 pound makes 50 cups) and the bridge method:

$$\frac{460 \text{ cups}}{1} \times \frac{1 \text{ pound}}{50 \text{ cups}} = \frac{460}{50} = 9.2 \text{ pounds of coffee needed to make 460 cups}$$

Step 5: Substitute these numbers into the total cost formula and multiply to find the total cost.

Total Cost = Number of Units × Cost per Unit =
9.2 pounds × $7.95/pound = $73.14

The total cost is $73.14.

Step 6: Round any partial pennies up to the next higher cent.
There are no partial pennies in this answer, so rounding is not necessary.

Step 7: Check the answer to make sure it is reasonable.

Example: A recipe calls for 1 1/2 teaspoons of dried tarragon leaves. One tablespoon of tarragon weighs .08 ounces. Tarragon is purchased in 4-ounce jars. Each jar costs $5.77. How much will the tarragon cost for this recipe?

Step 1: Read the problem and determine the quantity you are costing.

We need to find the cost of 1 1/2 teaspoons of tarragon.

Step 2: Identify the given as-purchased cost information.

Tarragon is sold by the jar for $5.77.

Step 3: Select the unit to be used for both the as-purchased cost and the quantity.

Since both the conversion and the cost are in ounces, it would make sense to choose ounces as the unit to solve this problem with.

Step 4: Perform the calculations necessary to convert the as-purchased cost and/or the quantity to the unit chosen in step 3.

The Quantity:

We can use the bridge method to convert the 1 1/2 teaspoons of tarragon to ounces, as described in Chapter 3.

$$\frac{1.5 \text{ teaspoons}}{1} \times \frac{1 \text{ tablespoon}}{3 \text{ teaspoons}} = \frac{1.5}{3} = .5 \text{ tablespoons}$$

$$\frac{.5 \text{ tablespoons}}{1} \times \frac{.08 \text{ ounces}}{1 \text{ tablespoon}} = .04 \text{ ounces}$$

The As-Purchased *Cost:*

To find the cost per ounce for tarragon, we will use the cost-per-unit formula:

$$\text{Cost per Unit} = \frac{\text{As-Purchased Cost}}{\text{Number of Units}} = \frac{\$5.77}{4 \text{ ounces}} = \$1.4425/\text{ounce}$$

Step 5: Substitute these numbers into the total cost formula and multiply to find the total cost.

Total Cost = Number of Units × Cost per Unit =
.04 ounces × $1.4225/ounce = $.0577

Step 6:   Round any partial pennies up to the next higher cent.

$.0577 rounds up to $.06

Step 7:   Check the answer to make sure it is reasonable.

When solving for total cost, any related unit may be selected to use in the equation. For the last problem, jars, teaspoons, tablespoons, ounces, or pounds could have been chosen. It usually requires fewer calculations to convert to a weight value (ounces or pounds). In addition, knowing the cost per ounce or pound of a given ingredient is more useful because it has many applications. Sometimes volume measure may be selected for the calculations if the product is bought and used in a volume quantity.

Conclusion

FINDING THE COST per unit and total cost for ingredients you will be using in the kitchen is needed for recipe costing which will be covered in Chapter 9. If you do not take the time to determine these amounts, you will be unable to properly estimate your cost for menu items produced in your kitchen. As a result, you will also be unable to find a selling price that will offer you a reasonable profit.

Chapter in Review

1. Find the cost per ounce and cost per can for a six-pack of soda (six 12-oz cans) that sells for $1.99.

2. Find the cost per ounce, cost per pound, and cost per head for a case of lettuce that costs $17 and contains 24 heads that weigh 26 oz each.

3. Find the cost per ounce and the cost per pound for smoked cheese that costs $20 for 5 lbs.

4. Find the cost per ounce and the cost per bottle for olive oil that comes in a case of six 1-gallon bottles and sells for $73.50 per case.

5. Find the cost per unit of the following items.

ITEM	PACK	AS-PURCHASED COST	COST PER UNIT
A. Asparagus	30#/crate	$87.90	_____ /#
B. Celery	30 bu/crate	$18.60	_____ /bu
C. Cucumber	48#(60 ea)/bushel	$13.92	_____ /ea
D. Escarole	18#(12 ea)/crate	$15.72	_____ /ea
E. Lettuce	24 head/crate	$17.00	_____ /head
F. Parsley	60 bu/bushel	$12.60	_____ /bu
G. Potatoes	50#	$12.00	_____ /#
H. Tomatoes, cherry	12 pt/cs	$16.96	_____ /pt

Find the cost per unit and the total cost for questions 13 and 14.

6. A 12-pound box of steaks is ordered, costing $6.99 per pound. If each steak weighs 6 ounces, what is the cost per steak, and how many steaks are in each box?

7. You want to serve 210 people each a 6-ounce portion of orange juice. Orange juice concentrate is purchased by the case for $22.80. Each case contains 12 cans, and each can makes 3/4 gallon. How much will the juice cost for the 210 people?

8. Calculate the cost of 1 pound of cumin if cumin is purchased in 12-ounce containers for $7.95.

9. How much would 1 cup of milk cost if you purchase milk by the gallon for $2.39?

10. If a 3.5-ounce portion of frozen spinach costs $.25, how much would a 5-pound box cost?

11. Bob bought 22 chickens. Each chicken weighs 3.5 pounds. The chickens cost Bob $81.62. How much did each chicken cost, and what is the cost per pound?

12. Twenty-five pounds of rice cost $18.00. One-half pound of rice was burned. What is the cost of the burned rice?

13. You purchase a case of dried cherries for $42.00. The case contains fourteen 12-ounce packages. What is the cost per pound? What is the cost per ounce?

14. A case of cornmeal costs $12.96. Each case contains 12 containers of cornmeal. If one container of cornmeal contains 1 pound 8 ounces of cornmeal, how much would 1 pound of cornmeal cost?

15. You make 12 cakes for a total cost of $35.52. Each cake is to be cut into 12 portions. How much does each cake cost you to make? How much does one slice of cake cost?

16. You are serving orange juice to a party of 170 people. Each person will receive a 6-ounce portion. You purchase orange juice by the half gallon for $1.69. How much will the 170 portions cost?

17. You purchase currant jelly for $22.20 per case. Each case contains 4 jars, and each jar contains 4 pounds of jelly. How much would a pound of jelly cost? How much would a half-ounce portion of jelly cost?

18. If you purchase 3 gallons of milk for $5.97, how much would 1 gallon cost? How much would 1 ounce cost? How much would 1 cup cost?

19. A box of shrimp (26–30/#) costs $34.95. Each box contains 5 pounds of shrimp. What is the cost per shrimp? (Use the lowest count to solve the problem.) What is the cost per pound of shrimp?

20. Six ounces of goat cheese costs $3.50. How much would 1 pound cost?

21. A recipe calls for 3 pounds of cornstarch. How much would 1 cup cost if cornstarch costs $.89 per pound? (1 C = 4.5 oz)

22. You are baking 48 loaves of cranberry bread. It takes 1/2 cup of fresh cranberries to make one loaf of cranberry bread. If cranberries cost $1.75 per pound, what will the cranberries cost for the 48 loaves of bread? (1 C = 6 oz)

23. How much would 1 teaspoon of cumin cost if 1 cup of cumin weighs 4 ounces and 1 pound of cumin is $10.60?

24. You are hosting a party for 25 people. A recipe for walnut bread serves 5 people and calls for 1/3 cup of walnuts. If 1 cup of walnuts weighs 4 ounces and walnuts are purchased for $3.50 a pound, how much will the walnuts cost for the party?

25. A recipe calls for 1/4 cup of chili powder. Chili powder is purchased in an 18-ounce container for $9.95. How much would the 1/4 cup of chili powder cost if 1 tablespoon of chili powder weighs .25 ounces?

26. How much would 1 3/4 cups of cocoa powder cost if cocoa powder is purchased in 50-pound bags for $45.57 and 1 tablespoon of cocoa powder weighs .25 ounces?

27. A 5-pound bag of cake flour costs $1.89. You are baking a cake that requires 3 1/2 cups of cake flour. What will the flour cost to make this cake?

CHAPTER 8

Edible Portion Cost

You are catering a party for 150 guests and the food order must be in by noon today. One of the side dishes that you plan to serve is potatoes au gratin. You need 33 pounds 12 ounces of peeled, sliced potatoes for this recipe; therefore, you must order a greater amount of whole, unpeeled potatoes to yield that quantity of peeled, sliced potatoes for the dish. If you purchased just 33 pounds 12 ounces of the whole, unpeeled potatoes, there would not be enough to make the correct amount of potatoes au gratin for the event.

Based on this example from Chapter 6, you can see that you have to purchase more than the amount of cleaned fresh fruit or vegetable listed in the recipe to compensate for the fact that it will be trimmed. The cost of the fruit or vegetable for any dish you prepare must include the cost of the trim, or else you will underestimate the expenses. This chapter investigates how cost is affected by the fact that you are purchasing more than you are using in the recipe.

Edible Portion Cost

CHAPTER 7 DISCUSSED how to use the yield percentage to determine how many potatoes to order so that there will be enough after they are cleaned and trimmed. This chapter examines how to determine the cost of the peeled potatoes for potatoes au gratin.

Hint

The Edible Portion Cost is always greater than the As-Purchased Cost if the yield percentage is less than 100%.

Definitions

The *as-purchased cost* (*APC*) is the cost paid to the supplier for the nonfabricated (uncleaned) fruit or vegetable. The *edible portion cost* (*EPC*) is the cost per unit of the fabricated (cleaned) fruit or vegetable. The EPC accounts not only for the cost of the fabricated product but also for the cost of the trim.

Formula for Edible Portion Cost

$$\text{Edible Portion Cost (EPC)} = \frac{\text{As-Purchased Cost (APC)}}{\text{Yield Percentage (in decimal form)}}$$

Steps to Calculate Edible Portion Cost for Ingredients with Less than 100% Yield

THE FOLLOWING STEPS will allow you to calculate the edible portion cost for any ingredient that must be trimmed.

1. Read the problem and identify the given as-purchased cost (APC) information.

2. Decide which unit to use and perform the calculations necessary to convert the as-purchased cost (APC) to this unit.

3. Find the yield percentage (pages 53–58).

4. Substitute the as-purchased cost (APC) and the yield percentage into the edible portion cost (EPC) formula and calculate the answer.

5. Make sure the answer is reasonable.

Caution

The yield percentage triangle shown in Chapter 6 is not designed to calculate cost. It is for calculating quantity only.

Finding Total Cost

Now THAT WE have the edible portion cost per unit, we need to apply the total-cost formula from Chapter 7.

1. Replace the number of units with the edible portion quantity.

2. Replace the cost per unit with the edible portion cost per unit.

3. Solve for the total cost.

Hint

To avoid making a mistake, pay attention to the edible portion cost number. If it is less than the as-purchased cost, something is very wrong. It will never cost less to have a cleaned amount of anything.

Total-Cost Formula

Total Cost = Edible Portion Quantity (EPQ) × Edible Portion Cost per Unit

Steps for Calculating the Total Cost Using the Edible Portion Cost

Use the following steps to calculate the total cost.

1. Calculate the edible portion cost (page 78).

2. Perform the calculation necessary so that the units for edible portion *quantity* and edible portion *cost per unit* are the same.

3. Insert the numbers into the total cost formula:

Total Cost = Edible Portion Quantity × Edible Portion Cost per Unit

4. Round any partial pennies up to the next higher cent.

5. Check the answer to make sure it is reasonable.

Example: You are purchasing broccoli for a party. In order to calculate the cost of the broccoli that will be served, the cost per pound must be determined. The broccoli was purchased by the bunch for $1.08. Broccoli has a 61 percent yield, and each bunch weighs 1.5 pounds. What is the edible portion cost per pound?

1. Read the problem and identify the given as-purchased cost information.

   The as-purchased cost is $1.08 per bunch.

2. Decide which unit of measure to use, and perform the calculations necessary to convert the as-purchased cost to this unit.

The problem asks for the cost per pound, so use the cost-per-unit formula to calculate the cost per pound for the broccoli.

$$\text{Cost per Unit} = \frac{\text{As-Purchased Cost}}{\text{Number of Units}} = \frac{\$1.08}{1.5 \text{ pounds}} = \$.72 \text{ per pound}$$

3. Find the yield percentage.

The yield percentage for broccoli is given in the problem as 61 percent.

4. Substitute the as-purchased cost and the yield percentage into the edible portion cost formula and calculate the answer.

$$\text{Edible Portion Cost} = \frac{\text{As-Purchased Cost}}{\text{Yield Percentage (in decimal form)}} =$$

$$\frac{\$.72 \text{ per pound}}{.61} = \$1.181 \text{ per pound, or } \$1.19$$

5. Make sure the answer is reasonable.

The result, $1.19 per pound of cleaned broccoli, does make sense, as it is higher than $.72 per pound.

In the problem above, it is not necessary to calculate the total cost because the question asks only for the edible portion cost for 1 pound.

Example: In the problem from the chapter introduction, 33.75# of peeled, sliced potatoes are needed for the potatoes au gratin. Potatoes cost $.32 per pound and have a yield percentage of 84 percent. Calculate the cost of the clean potatoes using both formulas: the edible portion cost formula and the total-cost formula.

1. Read the problem and identify the given as-purchased cost information.

The as-purchased cost is $.32 per pound.

2. Decide which unit of measure to use, and perform the calculations necessary to convert the as-purchased cost to the unit of choice.

In this problem, the obvious unit to stay with is pounds.

3. Find the yield percentage.

The yield percentage is given as 84 percent.

4. Substitute the as-purchased cost and the yield percentage into the edible portion cost formula.

$$\text{Edible Portion Cost} = \frac{\text{As-Purchased Cost}}{\text{Yield Percentage (in decimal form)}} =$$

$$\frac{\$.32 \text{ per pound}}{.84} = \$.3809 \text{ per pound}$$

5. Make sure the answer is reasonable.

The answer, $.3809 per pound, is greater than $.32 per pound, so it is reasonable.

Apply the edible portion cost to the total cost formula to find the cost of the clean potatoes.

1. Calculate the edible portion cost.

$.3809 per pound

2. Make sure that the units for edible portion quantity and edible portion cost per unit are the same.

In this problem the unit for both the quantity and the cost is pounds.

3. Insert the numbers into the total cost formula:

Total Cost = Edible Portion Quantity × Edible Portion Cost per Unit

33.75 pounds × $.3809 per pound = $12.8553

4. Round any partial pennies up to the next higher cent.

$12.8553 rounds up to $12.86.

5. Check the answer to make sure it is reasonable.

It makes sense that the cost of the 33.75 pounds of cleaned potatoes is $12.86.

Potatoes can be purchased already peeled and sliced. However, they cost more and may not be as fresh or as high quality. If potatoes were purchased already peeled and sliced, they would cost $.54 per pound. This is certainly more than $.3809 per pound. When a fruit or vegetable is bought already cleaned, the price will include the trim loss, extra packaging, and labor, among other costs.

This makes the cost of a cleaned product greater than the cost of an uncleaned product even though there would be costs attached to fabricating the potatoes yourself. This example also demonstrates that the edible portion cost will always be greater than or equal to the as-purchased cost.

Example: You are making a pesto sauce for a chicken dish you are preparing. You purchase basil in bunches. Each bunch weighs 2½ ounces and costs $.79 per bunch. One tablespoon of cleaned, chopped basil weighs .09 ounces, and basil has a 56 percent yield. How much will 1 cup of cleaned, chopped basil cost for this recipe?

1. Read the problem and identify the given as-purchased cost information.

   Basil is bought by the bunch for $.79.

2. Decide which unit of measure to use and perform the calculations necessary to convert the as-purchased cost to this unit.

   Because the weight is given in ounces, it is wise to stick with this unit and avoid unnecessary conversions.

   $$\text{Cost per Unit} = \frac{\text{As-Purchased Cost}}{\text{Number of Units}} = \frac{\$.79}{2.5 \text{ ounces}} = \$.316 \text{ per ounce}$$

3. Find the yield percentage.

   The yield percentage is given in the problem: 56 percent.

4. Substitute the as-purchased cost and the yield percentage into the edible portion cost formula and calculate the answer.

   $$\text{Edible Portion Cost} = \frac{\text{As-Purchased Cost}}{\text{Yield Percentage (in decimal form)}} =$$

   $$\frac{\$.316 \text{ per ounce}}{.56} = \$.5642$$

5. Make sure that the answer is reasonable.

   The edible portion cost, $.5642, is greater than the cost per unit, $.316, so it makes sense.

Now that you know the edible portion cost, use the steps for calculating the total cost and find out how much the cup of chopped fresh basil will cost.

1. Calculate the edible portion cost.

   We calculated the edible portion cost of the basil as $.5642 per ounce.

2. Perform the calculations necessary so that the edible portion quantity and the edible portion cost per unit use the same unit.

   The cost is in ounces, so, using the bridge method (Chapter 3), convert the cup of basil to ounces.

$$\frac{1 \text{ cup}}{1} \times \frac{16 \text{ tablespoons}}{1 \text{ cup}} = \frac{16 \text{ tablespoons}}{1} \times \frac{.09 \text{ ounces}}{.56} = 1.44 \text{ ounces}$$

3. Substitute the numbers into the total cost formula.

   Total Cost = Edible Portion Quantity × Edible Portion Cost per Unit

   1.44 ounces × $.5642 per ounce = $.8124

4. Round any partial pennies up to the next higher cent.

   The cost of the cup of chopped fresh basil is $.8124 or $.82.

5. Check the answer to make sure it is reasonable.

   Since an ounce of chopped fresh basil cost $.5642, it makes sense that 1.44 ounces costs a bit more.

Ingredients with 100 Percent Yield

MANY PRODUCTS HAVE a 100 percent yield, such as flour, sugar, dried spices, wines, spirits, syrups, and processed foods (see Figure 8.1). The edible portion cost may still be computed for these products, but we would be dividing by 1 (the decimal form of 100 percent), and any number divided by 1 equals itself. As a result, the edible portion cost and the as-purchased cost are the same.

FIGURE 8.1. These items are examples of ingredients with 100 percent yield.

When determining the cost of the meat or poultry that you fabricate, the terminology changes. For meat and poultry, we use the terms *new fabricated cost* and *new fabricated price per pound* instead of *edible portion cost*. The new fabricated price per pound recognizes the value of the trim that resulted from the fabrication process. Unlike fruits and vegetables, the trim from meat and poultry has a greater value, which needs to be taken into account when calculating the new fabricated price per pound.

$$\text{NEW FABRICATED PRICE PER POUND} = \frac{\text{NEW FABRICATED COST}}{\text{NEW FABRICATED WEIGHT}}$$

In the example from Chapter 6, you purchased a rib that weighs 36.9 pounds. The fat weighed 8 pounds, the bones weighed 7.3 pounds, and the usable trim weighed 8.7 pounds. The entire rib was originally purchased for $2.03 per pound. In Chapter 6, the new fabricated weight was calculated to be 12.9 pounds. The as-purchased cost was calculated by multiplying the as-purchased weight by the as-purchased price per pound:

$$36.9 \times \$2.03 = \$74.91$$

Step 1
To determine the value of the trim, check the current market prices with your purveyor. The following example is based on the following prices:
    fat: $.02 per pound
    bones: $.46 per pound
    usable trim: $2.45 per pound

For example, a jar of chili powder costs $5.15 per pound. A jar holds 1 pound. This entire product is usable, which makes the yield percentage 100 percent. In order to find the edible portion cost, you would divide $5.15 by 1 (the decimal form of 100 percent). Consequently, the edible portion cost ($5.15 per pound) and the as-purchased cost ($5.15 per pound) are the same.

Step 2

The total trim value is calculated by multiplying the number of pounds by the number of pound of each type of trim.

Fat: $.02 per pound × 8 pounds = $ .16

Bones: $.46 per pound × 7.3 pounds = $ 3.36

Usable Trim: $2.45 per pound × 8.7 pounds = $ 21.32

Total Trim Value $24.84

Step 3

To determine the new fabricated cost, subtract the total trim value from the as-purchased cost: $74.91 − $24.84 = $50.07

Step 4

To determine the new fabricated price per pound, substitute the new fabricated cost ($50.07) and the new fabricated weight (12.9 pounds) into the formula:

$$\text{New Fabricated Price per Pound} = \frac{\text{New Fabricated Cost}}{\text{New Fabricated Weight}}$$

$$= \frac{\$50.07}{12.9} = \$3.89 \text{ per pound}$$

This is the price you would use if you were costing a recipe with this particular fabricated meat as an ingredient.

Conclusion

THERE IS A SUBSTANTIAL amount of math involved in calculating the cost of ingredients that you will be using in the kitchen. It is imperative that you master this skill so that you may correctly determine the costs of your menu items and ultimately their selling prices.

Chapter in Review

Calculate the edible portion cost (EPC) per pound for the following items. For items marked with *, find the average weight per each before solving. See the Approximate Yield of Fruits and Vegetables chart on pages 59–60.

ITEM	APC	YIELD	EPC PER POUND
1. Beets, no tops	$0.37/#	76%	_____
2. Pineapples*	$2.93/ea	52%	_____
3. Cabbage, green	$0.45/#	79%	_____
4. Coconut*	$.50/ea	53%	_____
5. Celery*	$0.62/bu	75%	_____
6. Leeks*	$1.45/bu	52%	_____

7. You need 4.5 pounds of cleaned lettuce to make enough salad for a party of 20 people. Each head weighs 2.25 pounds and the yield percentage is 74 percent. A head of lettuce costs $.59. What is the cost of the lettuce for this party?

8. For a dessert you are making, you have purchased 4 pounds of raspberries at $3.29 per pound. When you prepare the raspberries, you have a 3 percent trim loss. How much would 1 pound of cleaned raspberries cost?

9. You have received new potatoes in the produce delivery. The as-purchased cost of the potatoes is $.75 per pound. If the yield on the potatoes is 81 percent, what is the edible portion cost per pound?

10. Chef Sharon made blueberry crêpes for a party of 27. Each crêpe contained 5 ounces of cleaned blueberries. The yield percentage for blueberries is 92 percent. If Chef Sharon bought blueberries in season for $1.80 per pound, how much would the blueberries cost for the party?

11. You purchase 20 pounds of onions for $23.80 and the yield percentage is 89 percent. What is the edible portion cost per pound for the onions?

12. The yield for strawberries is 87 percent. A pint of strawberries costs $1.92. How much would 1 cup of cleaned strawberries cost?

13. How much will 8 pints of cleaned raspberries cost if the as-purchased cost is $1.39 per pound? One cup of cleaned raspberries weighs 4.5 ounces and has a yield percentage of 97 percent.

14. You have just received 50 pounds of new potatoes. The invoice lists a price of $.75 per pound. If the yield percentage on new potatoes is 81 percent, what is the edible portion cost for 1 pound?

15. A recipe calls for 2 quarts of diced fresh tomatoes. If we purchase tomatoes for $1.09 per pound and the yield percentage is 90 percent, how much will the 2 quarts cost?

16. A recipe for banana pie calls for 3 cups of peeled, diced bananas. If bananas are purchased for $.79 per pound, how much will the 3 cups cost?

17. Why is the EPC always equal to or higher than the APC?

18. In what instances will the EPC be equal to the APC?

goals

- State the major reasons for a strong recipe pre-costing program
- Identify the components of a food cost form
- Cost out a recipe by completing a food cost form correctly
- Calculate the cost to produce a given recipe and the cost per portion
- Calculate an estimated selling price given an estimated food cost percentage

Recipe Costing

Chef Jean-Jacques opened a restaurant last year. The food was excellent, and the place was busy every night. Unfortunately, the restaurant closed eight months after it opened. What happened? An examination of the books revealed that the food was costing Jean-Jacques more than he thought, and as a consequence, he was not charging enough. Although the food was delicious and there were many loyal customers, Jean-Jacques did not control costs sufficiently, and the business could not survive. Excellence in the culinary arts is only one of the many skills necessary to be successful in the foodservice industry. One must also recognize the importance of the skills required to make a profit.

This chapter examines recipe costing, which is the basis of good food cost control.

Recipe Costing

THE TERM *FOOD COST* refers to the total cost of food items used in food production. Food cost does not include utensils, fuel for cooking, water, utilities, labor, or supplies. Food cost may be expressed as the cost of:

- A single item, such as a steak, a portion of fish, or a vegetable

- A single recipe, such as that for an entrée, soup, sauce, salad, bread, or cake

- Several items that make up a complete plate, such as a steak with potato, vegetable, and garnish

- Several components of a complete meal, such as bread and butter, soup, salad, entrée, dessert, and beverage

- Food items for a specific time period, such as breakfast, lunch, dinner, a day, a week, or a year

Any of the above examples may also be expressed in relation to the selling price of the item or the total food sales for a given period.

Definition

The food cost percentage (FC%) is the percentage of the selling price that pays for the ingredients.

The formula for the food cost percentage is:

$$\text{Food Cost Percentage} = \frac{\text{Food Cost}}{\text{Food Sales}} \text{ or } \frac{\text{Cost per Portion}}{\text{Selling Price}}$$

For example, the cost per portion of beef stew is $.92, and you are charging $4.00 per serving. Calculate the food cost percentage as follows:

$$\text{Food Cost Percentage} = \frac{\text{Cost per Portion}}{\text{Selling Price}} = \frac{\$.92}{\$4.00} = .23 \text{ or } 23\%$$

This indicates that 23 percent of the sales for beef stew pays for ingredients used to make it. What happens to the other 77 percent? The sales must also pay for the other expenses the operation incurred producing the beef stew: labor, utilities, and rent. Any remaining sales become profit.

Another way of looking at food cost is to relate it to a dollar. If a recipe has a 40 percent food cost, it may be said that the food cost is $0.40 for each $1.00 of sales.

The food cost percentage for an operation is a very important number. It is one of the tools used by management to evaluate profitability and menu items. Food cost for individual recipes, which is what this book examines, has two primary purposes for management: determining the selling price and forming the basis for a strong cost control program.

Determining Selling Price

ONCE YOU HAVE CALCULATED how much a recipe costs to make, the cost per portion can be calculated with the following formula:

$$\text{Cost per Portion} = \frac{\text{Total Recipe Cost}}{\text{Number of Portions}}$$

The cost per portion is then used to calculate the selling price based on a desired food cost percentage:

$$\text{Selling Price} = \frac{\text{Cost per Portion}}{\text{Food Cost Percentage (in decimal form)}}$$

There are many different ways to calculate the selling price for a menu item. The method addressed in this textbook is related to the mathematical formulas above. Other resources approach selling price from different avenues. These different methods should be researched before choosing menu prices.

A Strong Cost Control Program

DETERMINING FOOD COST through the use of food cost forms and comparing it to the actual food cost, which is based on inventory, is a good opportunity to make sure that the operation is running efficiently. If any discrepancies are found, the appropriate changes can be made.

The Arithmetic of Recipe Costing

TO ARRIVE AT AN ACCURATE COST of any menu item before it is produced, a standard recipe listing the ingredients and amounts, as well as the number of portions or servings desired, must be established. In addition, the following information must also be available:

1. The purchase unit and current market price of the ingredients (usually obtained from the supplier)

2. The yield percentage, to convert the as-purchased cost (APC) to the edible-portion cost (EPC). (See the Approximate Yield of Fruits and Vegetables chart on pages 59–60)

3. Volume-to-weight conversion formulas, to convert the ingredient's units and the purchase units when they do not correspond. (See the Approximate Volume to Weight chart on pages 45–47)

On the next page you will find a blank food cost form.

FOOD COST FORM

Menu Item _____ Date _____

Number of Portions _____ Size _____

Cost per Portion _____ Selling Price _____ Food Cost % _____

Ingredients	Recipe Quantity (EP)			Cost			Total Cost
	Weight	Volume	Count	APC/Unit	Yield %	EPC/Unit	
						Total Recipe Cost	

MENU ITEM: The name of the recipe identified as accurately as possible, using a menu number if necessary.

DATE: The day, month, and year the cost was calculated. This can be important for later analysis.

NUMBER OF PORTIONS: The number of portions the recipe makes or yields.

SIZE: The portion size normally served. This applies to menu items and is generally given in the recipe; it is not calculated.

COST PER PORTION: The cost of each serving. It is the total recipe cost divided by the number of portions.

SELLING PRICE: Based on the food cost percentage allowed by the budget. It is the cost per portion divided by the food cost percentage (in decimal form).

$$\text{Selling Price} = \frac{\text{Cost per Portion}}{\text{Food Cost Percentage (in decimal form)}}$$

FOOD COST %: An expression of food cost in relation to the selling price. It is the cost per portion divided by the selling price.

$$\text{Food Cost Percentage} = \frac{\text{Cost per Portion}}{\text{Selling Price}}$$

INGREDIENTS: All the food items that make up the recipe, including specific sizes or ID numbers.

RECIPE QUANTITY: This will be listed by weight, volume, or count depending on the recipe. The recipe quantity is usually the edible portion quantity. There are exceptions to this, which will be addressed in Chapter 11.

Recipe quantity is recorded in one of three ways:

• By weight—pounds, ounces, grams, etc.

• By volume—cups, pints, tablespoons, etc.

• By count—each, bunch, case, etc.

APC/UNIT: The as-purchased cost per unit is the current market price or the as-purchased price and the unit upon which price is based.

YIELD %: Many foods are not purchased already cleaned, and with these, some waste (trim) is expected. The yield percentage is used to adjust the as-purchased cost to compensate for trim loss.

EPC/UNIT: Edible portion cost per unit is the cost per unit of the fabricated fruit or vegetable. This cost accounts not only for the cost of the fabricated product but also for the trim loss. This is calculated by dividing the APC by the yield percentage (see Chapter 8).

$$\text{EPC} = \frac{\text{APC/Unit}}{\text{Yield Percentage (in decimal form)}}$$

If there is no waste or trim, the yield is 100 percent and this column may be left blank.

TOTAL COST: The total cost of each ingredient used.

TOTAL RECIPE COST: The sum of all items in the total cost column. This represents the total estimated cost of the recipe

Calculating Recipe Cost

CHAPTER 7 EXAMINED the total cost formula. This formula can be directly applied to the food cost form. Once again, the edible portion quantity and the as-purchased cost or edible portion cost must be converted to the same unit before multiplying them to calculate the total cost. The sample food cost chart on the following page gives the cost for the Grilled Herbed Salmon. Remember that this is only one method for finding the total cost of each ingredient, and that there are other possibilities. However, even if the math is done differently, your answer should be exactly the same.

To calculate the cost per portion, substitute the numbers into the formula:

$$\text{Cost per Portion} = \frac{\text{Total Recipe Cost}}{\text{Number of Portions}} = \frac{\$12.93}{10} = \$1.293 \text{ or } \$1.30 \text{ per portion}$$

To determine the selling price using the given food cost percentage, insert the numbers into the formula:

$$\text{Selling Price} = \frac{\text{Cost per Portion}}{\text{Food Cost Percentage}} = \frac{\$1.30}{.30} = \$4.3333 \text{ or } \$4.34$$

THE METHOD FOR CALCULATING TOTAL COST ON A FOOD COST FORM

1. Look at the units in each row, one row at a time, and decide what unit to use to solve the problem.

2. Convert the edible portion quantity and the as-purchased cost to the chosen unit.

3. Calculate the edible portion cost using the as-purchased cost and the yield percentage, if necessary.

4. Substitute the edible- portion quantity and the edible-portion cost per unit into total cost formula.

    Total Cost = Edible Portion Quantity × Edible Portion Cost/Unit

    Must be the same unit!

5. Round any partial pennies up to the next higher cent.

6. Make sure that the total cost for each ingredient makes sense.

THE METHOD FOR CALCULATING THE TOTAL RECIPE COST, COST PER PORTION, AND SELLING PRICE ON A FOOD COST FORM

1. Find the sum of the costs of all ingredients.
2. Find the cost per portion by dividing the total recipe cost by the number of portions.

$$\text{Cost per Portion} = \frac{\text{Total Recipe Cost}}{\text{Number of Portions}}$$

3. Determine the selling price by dividing the cost per portion by the food cost percent.

$$\text{Selling Price} = \frac{\text{Cost per Portion}}{\text{Food Cost Percentage (in decimal form)}}$$

FOOD COST FORM

Menu Item   Grilled Herbed Salmon   Date _____

Number of Portions 10   Size _____

Cost per Portion _____ Selling Price _____ Food Cost % 30%

Ingredients	Recipe Quantity (EP)			Cost			Total
	Weight	Volume	Count	APC/Unit	Yield %	EPC/Unit	**Cost**
1. Salmon filet	2¼#			$5.54/#	100%		
2. Lime juice (1 ea = 3.4 oz)		2 l		$.14/each	42%		
3. Parsley, chopped (1 bunch = 3.4 oz) (1 T = .075 oz)		2 T		$.49/bunch	52.9%		
4. Chives, chopped (1 bunch = 1 oz) (1 T = .1 oz)		2 T		$.67/bunch	100%		
5. Thyme, chopped (1 bunch = 1 oz) (1 T = .1 oz)		1 T		$.46/bunch	65%		
6. Black peppercorns, crushed (jar = 1#) (1 T = .231 oz.)		2 t		$9.11/jar	100%		
						Total Recipe Cost	

FOOD COST FORM

Menu Item: _Grilled Herbed Salmon_   Date _____

Number of Portions 10 _____   Size _____

Cost per Portion _____ Selling Price _____ Food Cost % _30%____

Ingredients	Recipe Quantity (EP)			Cost			Total Cost
	Weight	Volume	Count	APC/Unit	Yield %	EPC/Unit	
1. Salmon filet	$2\frac{1}{4}$#			$5.54/#	100%		$12.47

Solution using pounds:

$$2.25\# \times \$5.54/\# = \$12.465 \text{ or } \$12.47$$

Ingredients	Weight	Volume	Count	APC/Unit	Yield %	EPC/Unit	Total Cost
2. Lime juice (1 ea = 3.4 oz)		2 T		$.14/each	42%		$.10

Solution: 1 lime weighs 3.4 ounces. 1 tablespoon of lime juice weighs ½ ounce. Convert this row to ounces.

$$\frac{2T}{1} \times \frac{.5\,oz}{1T} = \textbf{1 ounce}$$

$$\frac{\$.14}{3.4\ oz} = \$.04/oz\ (APC)$$

$$\frac{\$.04/oz\ (APC)}{.42} = \textbf{\$.0952/oz (EPC)}$$

$$1\,oz\ \times \$.0952/oz = \$.0952\ or\ \$.10$$

Ingredients	Weight	Volume	Count	APC/Unit	Yield %	EPC/Unit	Total Cost
3. Parsley, chopped (1 bu = 3.4 oz) (1 T = .075 oz)		2 T		$.49/bunch	52.9%		$.05

Solution: convert this row to ounces using the given information.

$$\frac{2T}{1} \times \frac{.075\ oz}{1T} = \textbf{.15 ounce}$$

$$\frac{\$.49}{3.4\ oz} = \$.1441/oz\ (APC)$$

$$\frac{\$.1441}{.529} = \textbf{\$.2724/oz (EPC)}$$

$$.15\ oz. \times \$.2724/oz = \$.04086\ or\ \$.05$$

Ingredients	Weight	Volume	Count	APC/Unit	Yield %	EPC/Unit	Total Cost
4. Chives, chopped (1 bunch = 1 oz) (1 T = .1 oz)		2 T		$.67/bunch	100%		$.14

Solution: Both bunch and tablespoons can be converted to ounces.

$$\frac{2T}{1} \times \frac{.1\ oz}{1T} = \textbf{.2 oz}$$

$$\frac{\$.67}{1\ oz} = \textbf{\$.67/oz (APC)}$$

$$.2\ oz. \times 67/oz = \$.134\ or\ \$.14$$

Ingredients	Weight	Volume	Count	APC/Unit	Yield %	EPC/Unit	Total Cost
5. Thyme, chopped (1 bunch = 1 oz) (1 T = .1 oz)		1 T		$.46/bunch	65%		$.08

Solution: The weight of a tablespoon and the bunch is given in ounces. Convert both units to ounces.

$$1 T = \textbf{.1 oz}$$

$$\$.46/bunch\ (1\ oz)\ (APC)$$

$$\frac{\$.46}{.65} = \textbf{\$.7076/oz}\ (EPC)$$

$$.1\ oz. \times \$.7076/oz = \$.0707/oz\ or\ \$.08/oz$$

| 6. Black peppercorns, crushed (jar = 1#) (1 T = .231 oz.) | | 2 t | | $9.11/jar | 100% | | $.09 |

Solution: The weight of the tablespoon is in ounces and the weight of the jar is in pounds. It would be reasonable to convert to ounces or pounds. Convert the teaspoons to pounds and leave the APC alone.

$$\frac{2t}{1} \times \frac{1T}{3t} = \frac{.6666T}{1} \times \frac{.231\ oz}{1T} = \frac{.1539\ oz}{1} \times \frac{1\#}{16\ oz} = \frac{.1539}{16} = .0096\#$$

.0096# x $9.11/# = $.0874 or $.09

Add all the total costs to find the total recipe cost.

| | **Total Recipe Cost** | $12.93 |

FOOD COST FORM

Menu Item __Grilled Herbed Salmon_____ Date _____

Number of Portions 10_____ Size _____

Cost per Portion _____ *1.30* _____ Selling Price ____ *4.34* ____ Food Cost % __30%____

Ingredients	Recipe Quantity (EP)			Cost			Total
	Weight	Volume	Count	APC/Unit	Yield %	EPC/Unit	**Cost**
1. Salmon filet	2¼# 2.25#			$5.54/#	100%	$5.54/#	12.41
2. Lime juice (1 ea = 3.4 oz)	2l/1 x .50oz/1T =1oz	2 T		$.14/each $.14 = $.04oz / 3.4oz	42%	$.0952/oz	.10
3. Parsley, chopped (1 bunch = 3.4 oz) (1 T = .075 oz)	2T/1 x .075oz/1T = .150oz	2 T		$.49/bunch $.49 = $.144oz / 3.4oz	52.9%	$.2724/oz	.05
4. Chives, chopped (1 bunch = 1 oz) (1 T = .1 oz)	2T/1 x .1oz/1T = .20oz	2 T		$.67/bunch oz	100%	$.67/oz	.14
5. Thyme, chopped (1 bunch = 1 oz) (1 T = .1 oz)		1 T .1oz		$.46/bunch oz	65%	$.7016/oz	.08
6. Black peppercorns, crushed (jar = 1#) (1 T = .231 oz.)	2t/1 x 1T/3t = .6666T/1 x .231oz/1T =	2 t		$9.11/jar 1#	100%	$9.11/#	.09
	.1539oz/1 x 1#/16oz = .0096#						
						Total Recipe Cost	12.93

Conclusion

RECIPE COSTING is a critical part of the success that can be achieved in the food-service industry. Knowing the total cost, cost per portion, and the selling price of menu items will give you a tremendous advantage over your competitors, as well as managing your costs. This chapter is a culmination of all of the previous chapters. If you find you need more practice in any of the aspects of food costing found in this chapter, you should go back to and review the appropriate chapter.

Chapter in Review

COMPLETE THE FOLLOWING food cost forms to determine the total recipe cost, the cost per portion, and the selling price.

FOOD COST FORM

Menu Item Southwest White Bean Stew _____ Date _____

Number of Portions 10 servings _____ Size _____

Cost per Portion _____ Selling Price _____ Food Cost % _____ 25% _____

Ingredients	Recipe Quantity (EP)			Cost			Total
	Weight	Volume	Count	APC/Unit	Yield %	EPC/Unit	Cost
1. Navy beans, dried	14 oz			$.47/#	100%		
2. Chicken stock		2 qt		$2.00/G	100%		
3. Bouquet garni			1 ea	$.05 ea	100%		
4. Garlic, chopped (1 cup = 4.6 oz)		1.5 T		$1.73/#	88.1%		
5. Safflower oil (1 cup = 8 oz)		2 t		$2.35/33.8 oz	100%		
6. Red onion, diced	4 oz			$.40/#	90.6%		
7. Bell peppers, diced	4 oz			$.61/#	84.4%		
8. Jalapeño, seeded, diced	2 oz			$1.59/#	81.3%		
9. Garlic, minced	1 oz			$1.73/#	88.1%		
10. Cumin, ground (1 T =.208 oz)		1 T		$8.64/#	100%		
11. Sherry vinegar		2 fl oz		$3.54/33.8 oz	100%		
12. Tomato concassé (peeled, seeded, chopped)	4 oz			$1.73/#	78.4%		
13. Cilantro, chopped (1 bu = 2.8oz) (1 T = 0.86 oz)		2 T		$.32/bu	46.4%		
					Total Recipe Cost		

FOOD COST FORM

Menu Item   <u>Wild Mushroom and Nut Pie</u>   Date _____

Number of Portions <u>2 pies, 8 slices each</u>   Size <u>1 slice</u>

Cost per Portion _____   Selling Price _____   Food Cost %   <u>31.5%</u>

Ingredients	Recipe Quantity (EP)			Cost			Total Cost
	Weight	Volume	Count	APC/Unit	Yield %	EPC/Unit	
1. Dried cèpes	3/4 oz			$2.07/oz	100%		
2. Dried morels	3/4 oz			$4.31/oz	100%		
3. Almonds, chopped	7 oz			$2.59/#	100%		
4. Cashews, chopped	2 1/2 oz			$3.78/#	100%		
5. Butter (1 cup = 8 oz)		2 T		$2.66/#	100%		
6. Onion, diced	6 1/2 oz			$.20/#	90.6%		
7. Garlic, minced (1 C = 4.6 oz)		1 T		$1.73/#	88.1%		
8. White mushrooms, minced	8 oz			$1.45/#	93.8%		
9. Parsley, chopped (1 T =.075 oz) (1 bu = 3.4 oz)		2 T		$.49/bu	52.9%		
10. Marjoram, chopped (1 bu = 1 oz) (1 T = .058 oz)		1 T		$.38/bu	76%		
11. Thyme, chopped (1 bu = 1 oz) (1 T = .075 oz.)		2 t		$.46/bu	65%		
12. Sage, chopped (1 bu = 1 oz) (1 T = .075 oz.)		1 t		$.45/bu	60%		
13. Brown rice, raw	6 oz			$1.25/#	100%		
14. Fontina cheese	6 oz			$7.33/#	100%		
15. Mozzarella cheese	3 oz			$3.01/#	100%		
16. Whole eggs			2 ea	$.82/doz	100%		
						Total Recipe Cost	

FOOD COST FORM

Menu Item Braised Lamb Shanks with Lentils _____ Date _____
Number of Portions 10 servings _____ Size _____
Cost per Portion _____ Selling Price _____ Food Cost % 27%

Ingredients	Recipe Quantity (EP)			Cost			Total Cost
	Weight	Volume	Count	APC/Unit	Yield %	EPC/Unit	
1. Lamb shanks	40 oz			$1.98/#	100%		
2. Salt (1 box = 1# 10 oz) (1 T = ²/₃ oz)		½ t		$.38/box	100%		
3. Black pepper, ground (1 T = ¼ oz)		¼ t		$6.07/#	100%		
4. Vegetable oil		2 T		$6.40/qt	100%		
5. Fond de veau lié		1 qt		$3.00/qt	100%		
6. White wine, dry		1 pt		$4.02/50.7 oz	100%		
7. Bouquet garni			1 ea	$.05/ea	100%		
8. Lentils, green	12 oz			$.43/#	100%		
9. Celery, diced (1 bu = 32 oz)	8 oz			$.62/bu	68.8%		
10. Carrots, diced	8 oz			$.33/#	81.3%		
11. Parsley, chopped (1 T = .075 oz) (1 bu = 3.4 oz)		2 T		$.49/bu	52.9%		
12. Orange juice		1½ T		$2.60/G	100%		
13. Thyme, chopped (1 T = .1 oz) (1 bu = 1 oz)		1 T		$.46/bu	65%		
						Total Recipe Cost	

FOOD COST FORM

Menu Item ___Grilled Soft-Shell Crabs_____ Date _____

Number of Portions ___10 servings_____ Size _____

Cost per Portion _____ Selling Price _____ Food Cost % ___34%_____

Ingredients	Recipe Quantity (EP)			Cost			Total Cost
	Weight	Volume	Count	APC/Unit	Yield %	EPC/Unit	
1. Red wine vinegar		14 fl oz		$1.07/34 oz	100%		
2. Dry white wine		14 fl oz		$4.02/50.7 oz	100%		
3. Olive oil, extra virgin		3 fl oz		$4.42/17 oz	100%		
4. Red pepper, minced	2 oz			$2.99/#	84.4%		
5. Scallions, minced (1 C = 2 oz) (1 bu = 3.5 oz)	2 oz			$.26/bu	82.9%		
6. Jalapeños, peeled, seeded, chopped	1 oz			$1.59/#	81.3%		
7. Garlic, minced (1 C = 4.6 oz)		2 T		$1.73/#	88.1%		
8. Basil, chopped (1 bu = 2.5 oz) (1 T = .088 oz)		1 T		$.56/bu	56%		
9. Fennel tops, chopped (1 cup = 3 oz)		1 T		$.98/#	92%		
10. Tarragon, chopped (1 bu = 1 oz) (1 T = .114 oz)		1 T		$.48/bu	80%		
11. Thyme, chopped (1 bu = 1 oz) (1 T = .1 oz)		1 T		$.46/bu	65%		
12. Soft-shell crabs, large, cleaned			10 ea	$2.43/ea	100%		
					Total Recipe Cost		

CHAPTER 10

Applying Yield Percentage in the Kitchen

You have been hired to cater a party for 150 people and will be making your famous apple pie. Your calculations show that you'll need 52 1/2 pounds of apples to make the 15 pies necessary to serve 150 people. Would it be reasonable to order 52 1/2 pounds of apples? If you ordered that quantity of apples and then peeled, cored, and sliced them, the cleaned apples would weigh significantly less, and there would not be enough apples to make the pies. It is important to remember that the trim loss—in this case, the peels and cores—must be taken into account when ordering any fresh fruit or vegetable. An accurate prediction of the amount of fruit needed would eliminate the possibility of over- or underordering.

This chapter investigates the use of yield percentage and how it would be used to solve this situation and others like it.

Calculating the As-Purchased Quantity

IT IS NECESSARY to consider the trim loss when purchasing items, but many recipes list ingredients in edible portion amounts. If you confuse the as-purchased quantity with the edible portion quantity, the recipe may not work, or it may not yield the number of portions desired. The edible portion quantity must be converted to the as-purchased quantity, for purchasing. Using the yield percentage, this can be calculated.

$$\text{As-purchased quantity (APQ)} = \frac{\text{Edible Portion Quantity (EPQ)}}{\text{Yield Percentage (in decimal form)}}$$

Example: It has already been determined that 52 1/2 (52.5) pounds of cleaned apples are needed to make the apple pies for the party discussed in the chapter introduction. The formula above can be applied to this situation to calculate the amount of apples that should be ordered to make the 15 pies. Apples have a 76 percent yield:

> **Rounding**
>
> **When rounding amounts to order, always round up. If the amount is rounded down, the order quantity would be underestimated.**

$$\text{APQ} = \frac{\text{EPQ}}{\text{Yield Percentage}} = \frac{52.5 \text{ pounds}}{.76} = 69.07 \text{ pounds (APQ) or } 70 \text{ pounds}$$

The minimum amount of apples that should be ordered to be sure that there are enough apples for the pies is 70 pounds.

Yield percentage takes into account only the trim loss that occurs during fabrication of the apples. There are other losses that may occur, such as:

- Theft
- Spoilage
- Excessive waste (the yield percentage may not really be 76 percent), due to the poor skill level of the person fabricating the product or a lack of quality in the product
- Mistakes in the kitchen, including burning, dropping, or contamination

FIGURE 10.1. **Although a yield chart is helpful, a foodservice professional must keep in mind how an item will be used in a dish. If only the florets of the broccoli are being used, the yield percentage is much lower than if the stalks would also be used.**

The APQ can be calculated precisely, but it is important to remember that human and other uncontrollable errors may occur in a commercial kitchen and need to be considered (see Figure 10.1).

When the Yield Is 100 Percent

IT SHOULD BE KEPT IN MIND that not all foods have a trim loss. Many foods have 100 percent yield, such as sugar, flour, or dried spices. Other foods have a yield percentages that can change, depending on how they are served. These circumstances and others will be addressed in Chapter 11.

Calculating the Edible Portion Quantity

SOMETIMES IT IS NECESSARY to determine how many portions can be created from the as-purchased quantity. The amount of cleaned product (edible portion quantity) that can be obtained from a purchased item can be determined using the formula below. Once the edible portion quantity has been calculated, the number of portions that can be obtained can be calculated.

Edible Portion Quantity = As-Purchased Quantity (APQ) × Yield Percentage (in decimal form)

Example: You purchased a case of fresh green beans that weighs 20 pounds. How many .25-pound servings of cleaned green beans are in the case? First look up the yield percentage for green beans, which is 88 percent, and then compute the weight of the beans after cleaning.

Edible portion quantity = APQ × Yield Percentage

Edible portion quantity = 20 pounds × .88 = 17.6 pounds

The calculation shows that the edible portion quantity would be 17.6 pounds. Now you can calculate how many .25-pound portions of cleaned green beans can be served from 17.6 pounds of cleaned green beans.

$$\text{Number of Servings} = \frac{\text{Edible Portion Quantity}}{\text{Portion Size}}$$

Rounding

The number of portions should be rounded down, since it would not be feasible to serve a partial portion to a guest

$$\text{Number of Servings} = \frac{17.6 \text{ pounds}}{.25 \text{ pounds}} = 70.4$$

You should be able to obtain 70 full servings from the case of green beans.

The EPQ/APQ/Yield Percentage Triangle

THIS TRIANGLE was introduced in Chapter 6 as a tool to find the yield percentage, as-purchased quantity, and edible portion quantity. It is mathematically identical to the part/whole/percentage triangle introduced in Chapter 2; the only difference is in the terms used. So, do not think of this as ANOTHER tool to learn, think of it as a variation of what you already know.

> Part = Edible Portion Quantity
> Whole = As-Purchased Quantity
> Percent = Yield Percentage

EPQ/APQ/Y% (Yield Percentage) Triangle Directions

1. Determine what you are looking for: EPQ, APQ, or yield percentage.

2. *To find the edible portion quantity (EPQ):*

   Cover the EPQ for edible portion quantity.

   APQ and Y% are side by side. This directs you to multiply the APQ by the yield percentage. (Remember to change the percentage to a decimal by dividing by 100.)

   To find the as-purchased quantity (APQ):

   Cover the APQ for as-purchased quantity.

   EPQ is over Y%. This directs you to divide the EPQ by the yield percentage. (Remember to change the percentage to a decimal by dividing by 100.)

   To find the yield percentage:

   Cover the Y% for yield percentage.

   EPQ is over APQ. This directs you to divide the EPQ by the APQ and multiply the answer by 100 to convert it to the yield percentage.

Conclusion

YIELD PERCENTAGE is a useful tool for a professional chef. Mastering this concept will allow you to approach purchasing decisions in a logical and organized manner. In addition, you will also handle the determination of the number of portions that can be prepared from a particular amount of product.

Chapter in Review

Solve the following problems. If necessary, refer to the Approximate Yield of Fruits and Vegetables chart on pages 59–60.

1. You are serving 3-ounce portions of fresh green beans to 150 guests. How many pounds of green beans should you purchase?

2. A recipe for baba ghannuj (puréed roasted eggplant) requires 1 1/2 ounces of puréed eggplant for each serving. If you make enough baba ghannuj to serve 300 people, how many eggplants should you purchase?

3. You need two hundred and fifty 5-ounce portions of fresh pineapple. How many pineapples should you purchase?

4. You have a case of green cabbage. Each case contains 15 cabbages. If you want to provide 2 1/2-ounce servings, how many servings can be obtained from the case?

5. How many coconut pies can be made from 25 coconuts if each pie contains 1.375 pounds of coconut?

For questions 6–13, calculate the as-purchased quantity (APQ). Note: Starred items (*) are usually purchased singly or by the bunch. See the Approximate Yield of Fruits and Vegetables chart on pages 59–60.

	RECIPE ITEM	RECIPE QUANTITY	YIELD %	AS-PURCHASED QUANTITY
6.	Bananas, sliced	5# 6 oz		
7.	Blackberries	15#		
8.	Broccoli, trimmed*	7 1/2#		/bunch
9.	Nectarines	6#12 oz		
10.	Celery, julienned*	1 3/4#		/bunch
11.	Plums, pitted	8#		
12.	Garlic, finely diced	2 oz		
13.	Pineapple*	10#		/each

14. The chef has asked you to prepare one hundred and six 6-ounce portions of broccoli florets. If the yield for broccoli when making florets is 60 percent, how many bunches of broccoli do you need to purchase?

15. You purchase a bushel of spinach, which weighs 25 pounds. How many 4-ounce portions can you obtain from the bushel?

16. Forty people are coming for lunch and you are serving each a 4-ounce portion of potatoes. One bag of red potatoes weighs 52 pounds. After peeling and trimming, the potatoes weigh 47 pounds 7 ounces. How many pounds of red potatoes will be left after lunch is served?

17. If you purchase 6 bunches of celery, each weighing 2 pounds 1 ounce, and the yield percentage is 75 percent, how many 2-ounce servings can be made?

18. Joe has KP duty. He is given 2,000 pounds of potatoes to peel. If the yield percentage is 81 percent, how many 5-ounce portions will he have?

19. Tammy is having a party for 100 people. She is serving okra and has purchased 25 pounds. If the yield percentage is 79 percent, what size portion will each guest receive?

20. You have 12 pounds 6 ounces of Brussels sprouts. How many 3-ounce servings can be made if the yield percentage is 74 percent?

21. How many 3.25-ounce portions of eggplant can be obtained from 16 eggplants weighing 1.25# each, if the yield percentage is 95 percent?

22. Chef Howard has 30 pounds of cleaned chicken breasts for chicken cordon gold. How many pounds of chicken were purchased if the yield percentage is 67 percent?

23. For a banquet of 480 people you are to prep 2 1/2-ounce portions of broccoli. You obtain 30 pounds of cleaned broccoli. How much more broccoli must you purchase to complete the prep for the banquet if the yield percentage is 61 percent?

24. For every 30 pounds of green beans you purchase, you end up with 26 pounds of cleaned green beans. What is the yield percentage for green beans? How many pounds should you order if you need 50 pounds of cleaned green beans?

CHAPTER **11**

Special Topics

goals

- Identify the circumstances when the yield percentage does not need to be taken into account when calculating the as-purchased quantity

- Identify the circumstances when the yield percentage does not need to be taken into account when calculating the edible portion cost

You will be making pear sorbet for a party that you are catering on the last Saturday of this month. The next day, you will be making poached pears, and you would like to order the pears for these two events in advance.

The pear sorbet requires 15.75 pounds of peeled, cored, and diced pears for the 84 guests to be served. To determine the amount that needs to be ordered, divide the edible portion quantity by the yield percentage, as discussed in Chapter 10 From the yield chart, you know that the yield percentage for pears is 76 percent. So 15.75 pounds ÷ .76 = 20.72 or 21 pounds. You should order 21 pounds of pears for this recipe.

The poached pears require 36 pears for the 36 portions. An average pear weighs 7 ounces, as purchased. Multiply to calculate the number of pounds of pears needed to equal 36 pears: 36 × 7 ounces = 252 ounces or 15.75 pounds of pears. How many pounds of pears will have to be ordered for this event? Would yield percentage be used in this situation?

When to Use Yield Percentage

WHEN IS THE YIELD PERCENTAGE used to calculate the amount to order?

For the sorbet mentioned in the introduction to the chapter, 15.75 pounds of cleaned pears are needed. Unless pears are being bought cleaned and trimmed, waste must be accounted for by dividing the edible portion quantity by the yield percentage (see Chapter 10) because the pear must be fabricated before it is used.

FIGURE 11.1. Yield percentage, although important in estimating the as-purchased quantity, must be considered in the context of the recipe. Knowing how the item is to be used is very important in determining the amount to purchase. The quantity of pears for the sorbet (*left*) is quite different than that for the poached pear recipe (*right*).

In recipes such as that for poached pears, 36 pears are needed to serve 36 people (see Figure 11.1). Should yield percentage be used in this case? No, because the recipe calls for 1 pear per portion.

If a recipe lists an ingredient that has less than 100 percent yield by count, it is most likely not necessary to use the yield percentage. For example, if a recipe calls for 3 cloves of garlic, it is not necessary to have more than 3 cloves to account for waste even though garlic does not have a 100 percent yield. In this recipe the garlic is called for in the as-purchased quantity; therefore yield percentage should not be taken into account. (See page 114 for exceptions.)

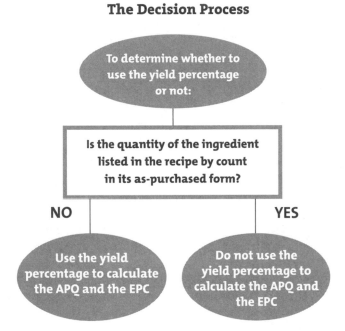

The Decision Process

To determine whether to use the yield percentage or not:

Is the quantity of the ingredient listed in the recipe by count in its as-purchased form?

NO

YES

Use the yield percentage to calculate the APQ and the EPC

Do not use the yield percentage to calculate the APQ and the EPC

What Happens to Cost?

SIMILAR TO CALCULATING as-purchased quantity, when a recipe calls for ingredients by the piece or each, it will affect the way cost is calculated. In Chapter 8, the as-purchased cost was changed to the edible portion cost to take trim loss into account. When costing a recipe that has ingredients listed in quantities that would be placed in the count column on a food cost form, that amount is actually, with a few exceptions (discussed below), the as-purchased quantity. Therefore, there is no need to use the yield percentage to calculate the edible portion cost because it is not necessary to buy more product to compensate for the trim loss.

Let's apply what we just discussed to food costing. Using the pear examples, we will cost out the pears for each recipe.

Ingredients	Recipe Quantity (EP)			Cost			Total Cost
	Weight	Volume	Count	APC/Unit	Yield %	EPC/Unit	
Pears (for sorbet)	15.75#			$.75/#	76%	.75 ÷ .76 = $.9868/#	15.75# x $.9868/# = $15.55
Pears (for poached pears) (1 ea = 7 oz)			36 ea 36 ea x 7 oz = 252 oz ÷ 16 oz = 15.75#	$.75/#	~~76%~~	$.75/#	15.75# x $.75 = $11.82

Notice that even though the weight of the pears is the same in both recipes, the cost is different. The main difference is that the weight of the pears for the sorbet is an edible portion quantity and the weight of the pears for the poached pears is an as-purchased quantity; the math must be different to reflect this difference.

The Exception to the Exception

THERE ARE TYPES OF INGREDIENTS that may be listed in the count column on a food cost form that nevertheless require the use of the yield percentage.

Hint

When a food cost form already has the information on it, look over the form before beginning to cost. If there are any ingredients in the count column, be careful—you may not have to use yield percentage to calculate the edible portion cost.

This situation occurs when a recipe calls for a cut of an ingredient in its edible portion form, such as 10 melon balls, 6 tournée-cut carrots, and the like. These cuts most definitely require a yield percentage since they will not be purchased prefabricated.

Conclusion

THERE ARE MANY DIFFERENT WAYS of writing recipes. A recipe can call for 1 pound of cleaned onions or 2 medium onions. The final product of the recipe will be more consistent if the ingredients are listed by weight or volume because there are no absolute definitions as to what qualifies as a medium onion or a medium potato, whereas weight and volume measures are precisely defined: 1 cup of diced onion, 1 pound of peeled potatoes.

Chapter in Review

Complete the following chart for questions 1–4.

THE SITUATION	USE THE YIELD PERCENTAGE?	WHY OR WHY NOT?
1. A recipe calls for 6 cups of diced pears.		
2. A recipe calls for 2 medium onions, peeled and diced.		
3. A recipe calls for 2 tablespoons of chopped garlic, but you are buying garlic by the bulb.		
4. The recipe calls for 1 bunch of parsley, chopped.		

5. You are making broccoli quiche for 200 people. Each serving requires 2.5 ounces of cleaned broccoli. The yield percentage for broccoli is 61 percent. How many pounds of broccoli should you order?

6. You are serving pasta with broccoli for 100 people. One bunch of broccoli will serve 8 people. How many pounds of broccoli will you need to order if the yield for broccoli is 61 percent? (1 bunch = 1.5 pounds)

7. You need 3 pounds of trimmed pears to make 4 tarts. How many pounds of pears must be purchased if the yield percentage is 78 percent?

8. Poached pears with brandy sauce will be the dessert for tonight's buffet. If each case contains 48 pears, how many cases will be needed if each of the 300 guests will be served 1 pear for dessert and pears have a yield percentage of 78 percent?

9. You are making caramel apples for 12 people. If each apple weighs approximately 10 ounces and the yield percentage for apples is 76 percent, how many pounds of apples do you need to order?

10. You need 389 stuffed green peppers. Each green pepper weighs 7 ounces. If a case of green peppers weighs 25 pounds, how many cases of green peppers should be ordered if the yield percentage for peppers is 82 percent?

11. You are making 12 vegetarian pizzas. Each pizza contains 2 cups of chopped green peppers. Each pepper weighs 7 ounces, and 1 cup of peppers weighs 5.2 ounces. If a green pepper has a yield percentage of 82 percent, how many peppers should you purchase?

12. You are having a dinner party for 15 people, and one item on the menu is avocado-and-grapefruit salad. Each salad calls for 1/3 of an avocado and 1/2 of a grapefruit, both peeled and seeded. How many avocados and grapefruits will you need if the yield percentage for avocados is 60 percent and for grapefruit 50 percent?

In the following food cost form, the yield percentages are given for each of the ingredients. Determine if the yield percentage needs to be used to calculate the cost of each ingredient as you complete the form.

Food Cost Form

Menu Item <u>Stir-Fried Vegetables</u> Date _____
Number of Portions <u>10</u> Size _____
Cost per Portion _____ Selling Price _____ Food Cost % <u>25%</u>

Ingredients	Recipe Quantity (EP)			Cost			Total Cost
	Weight	Volume	Count	APC/Unit	Yield %	EPC/Unit	
13. Onion, diced (1 cup = 6^{1}/$_{2}$ oz)		2 cups		$.40/#	89%		
14. Red peppers, sliced (1 each = 5 ^{1}/$_{3}$ oz)			3 each	$3.99/#	86%		
15. Green pepper, sliced	1# 5oz			$.90/#	85%		
16. Carrots, diced	1#			$.98/#	82%		
17. Celery, sliced (1 bunch = 2#)			1 bunch	$1.69/bu	75%		
18. Garlic, minced (1 bulb =3 oz) (1 bulb = 13 cloves)			3 cloves	$2.69/#	79%		
19. Ginger root, minced	^{1}/$_{2}$oz			$3.89/#	65%		
20. Sesame oil		1 tsp		$9.18/64 oz	100%		
21. Soy sauce (1 bottle = 5 oz)		1 cup		$1.25/bottle	100%		
22. Five-spice powder (1 cup = 3 oz)		^{1}/$_{2}$ tsp		$8.95/12 oz	100%		
23. Sesame seed (1 cup = 4 oz)		2 tbsp		$.89/#	100%		
24. Scallions, chopped (1 cup = .1875#) (1 bunch = 5 oz)		1^{1}/$_{2}$ cups		$.59/bu	85%		
					Total Recipe Cost		

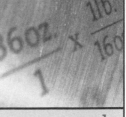

Recipe Size Conversion

You are a private chef and must accommodate many parties of varying sizes. Next week there are two parties scheduled. The first party is for 12 people. The hostess wants to serve a recipe you created, but it yields 40 portions. For the other party scheduled, she has requested onion soup. Your recipe yields 2 gallons, but you need the recipe to yield ten 5-ounce portions. Converting recipe yields can become tricky. There are certain steps that may be followed to ease this type of yield conversion while still maintaining the integrity of the original recipe.

FIGURE 12.1. **Flexibility in converting recipe sizes is essential in the professional kitchen.**

Converting Recipe Yields

RECIPES PRODUCE a specific yield in the form of weight, volume, or count. For example, a recipe can yield 3 pounds of bread dough, 2 gallons of tomato soup, or 12 servings of baked apple dessert. Often it is necessary to alter the yield of a recipe to accommodate particular needs (see Figure 12.1).

For example:

ORIGINAL RECIPE YIELD	NEW RECIPE YIELD
3 pounds of bread dough	20 pounds of bread dough
2 gallons of tomato soup	4 1/2 gallons of tomato soup
12 servings of baked apple dessert	50 servings of baked apple dessert

To convert the yield of a recipe, there are several steps that should be followed to ensure that the product will have the same taste and texture as the original recipe. The most direct method is to first calculate a recipe conversion factor (RCF). This factor may be used to adjust the ingredient quantities in the original recipe to fit the desired yield.

Calculating the Recipe Conversion Factor (RCF)

A RECIPE CONVERSION FACTOR (RCF) is a number that represents the relationship between the new and old recipe yields.

The three **NOs** of calculating RCFs:

1. $\dfrac{\text{New Recipe Yield}}{\text{Old Recipe Yield}} = \dfrac{N}{O} = $ Recipe Conversion Factor

   * be careful not to invert this—you will get ON instead of NO!

2. **NO** rounding of the recipe conversion factor

3. **NO** units—the recipe conversion factor carries no unit

Calculating RCF with the Same Units

ORIGINAL RECIPE YIELD	NEW RECIPE YIELD
1. 3 pounds of bread dough	20 pounds of bread dough
2. 2 gallons of tomato soup	4 1/2 gallons of tomato soup
3. 12 servings of baked apple dessert	50 servings of baked apple dessert

1. bread dough:

$$\frac{\text{New}}{\text{Old}} = \frac{20 \, \cancel{\text{pounds}}}{3 \, \cancel{\text{pounds}}} = \frac{20}{3} = 6.6666$$

2. tomato soup:

$$\frac{\text{New}}{\text{Old}} = \frac{4.5 \, \cancel{\text{gallons}}}{2 \, \cancel{\text{gallons}}} = \frac{4.5}{2} = 2.25$$

3. baked apple dessert:

$$\frac{\text{New}}{\text{Old}} = \frac{50 \, \text{servings}}{12 \, \text{servings}} = \frac{50}{12} = 4.166$$

> ### Note
>
> When the recipe conversion factor is found, there is no unit attached to it. This number is a factor—a unitless number. For example, if you were to double a recipe, you would multiply all the ingredients by 2. The 2 is the RCF, which has no unit.

In the above examples, the new recipe yield and the old recipe yield have the same unit. This is not always the case.

Calculating RCF with Different Units

A recipe yields 3 quarts of soup, and the yield needs to be changed to 2 gallons. In this type of situation, in which the units are not the same, the calculations will be the same as shown with one additional step: Before you calculate the RCF, the unit in the old recipe must match the unit in the new recipe.

$$\frac{\text{New}}{\text{Old}} = \frac{2 \, \text{gallons}}{3 \, \text{quarts}} = \frac{2 \, \cancel{\text{gallons}}}{.75 \, \cancel{\text{gallon}}} = 2.666$$

$$\frac{3 \, \cancel{\text{qt}}}{1} \times \frac{1 \, \text{gallon}}{4 \, \cancel{\text{qt}}} = \frac{3}{4} = .75 \, \text{gallon}$$

or

Another way to find RCF for this problem is to convert all to quarts.

$$\frac{\text{New}}{\text{Old}} = \frac{2\,\text{gallons}}{3\,\text{quarts}} = \frac{8\,\cancel{\text{quarts}}}{3\,\cancel{\text{quarts}}} = 2.666$$

$$\frac{2\,\cancel{\text{gallons}}}{1} \times \frac{4\,\text{quarts}}{1\,\cancel{\text{gallon}}} = 8\,\text{quarts}$$

Whether all the units are converted to quarts or to gallons, the result is the same.

Let's take some additional examples:

ORIGINAL RECIPE YIELD	NEW RECIPE YIELD
1. 1 cup of sauce	1 quart of sauce
2. 1 1/2 pounds of spice mix	12 ounces of spice mix
3. 1 1/2 pints of salsa	1 3/4 gallons of salsa

1. Sauce

$$\frac{\text{New}}{\text{Old}} = \frac{1\,\text{quart}}{1\,\text{cup}} = \frac{4\,\cancel{\text{cups}}}{1\,\cancel{\text{cup}}} = 4$$

$$\frac{1\,\cancel{\text{qt}}}{1} \times \frac{4\,\text{cups}}{1\,\cancel{\text{qt}}} = 4\,\text{cups}$$

Note

This problem could also be solved by converting all the units to quarts. The result would be the same.

2. Spice mix

$$\frac{\text{New}}{\text{Old}} = \frac{12\,\text{ounces}}{1\,1/2\,\text{pounds}} = \frac{.75\,\cancel{\text{pound}}}{1.5\,\cancel{\text{pounds}}} . = .5$$

$$\frac{12\,\cancel{\text{ounces}}}{1} = \frac{1\,\text{pound}}{16\,\cancel{\text{ounces}}} = \frac{12}{16} = .75\,\text{pounds}$$

Note

This problem could also be solved by converting all the units to ounces. The result would be the same.

3. Salsa

$$\frac{\text{New}}{\text{Old}} = \frac{1\,3/4\,\text{gallons}}{1\,1/2\,\text{pints}} = \frac{14\,\cancel{\text{pints}}}{1.5\,\cancel{\text{pints}}} = 9.333$$

$$\frac{1.75\,\cancel{\text{gallons}}}{1} \times \frac{8\,\text{pints}}{1\,\cancel{\text{gallon}}} = \frac{14}{1} = 14\,\text{pints}$$

Note

This problem could also be solved by converting all the units to gallons. The result would be the same.

Calculating RCF with Portion Sizes

In the following examples, all the ingredients must first be converted to one unit.

ORIGINAL RECIPE YIELD	NEW RECIPE YIELD
1. 30 5-ounce portions wild rice soup	150 6-ounce portions wild rice soup
2. 50 1/4-cup servings mango salsa	2 gallons mango salsa
3. 36 6-ounce oatmeal raisin cookies	5 1/2 dozen 2-ounce oatmeal raisin cookies

In each case, the ingredient quantities must be converted to the same unit before the RCF can be calculated. This may require some additional steps.

1. Wild rice soup

$$\frac{\text{New}}{\text{Old}} = \frac{150 \text{ 6-ounce portions}}{30 \text{ 5-ounce portions}} =$$

$$\frac{150 \times 6 \text{ ounces}}{30 \times 5 \text{ ounces}} = \frac{900 \text{ ounces}}{150 \text{ ounces}} = 6$$

> **Note**
>
> Using the 150 portions and the 30 portions to calculate the RCF in the above problem will only work if the portion sizes are the same (both 5-ounce portions or both 6-ounce portions).

2. Mango salsa

$$\frac{\text{New}}{\text{Old}} = \frac{2 \text{ gallons}}{50 \times 1/4 \text{ cup}} = \frac{2 \text{ gallons}}{12 \ 1/2 \text{ cup}} =$$

$$\frac{32 \text{ cups}}{12 \ 1/2 \text{ cups}} = 2.56$$

3. Oatmeal raisin cookies

$$\frac{\text{New}}{\text{Old}} = \frac{5 \ 1/2 \text{ dozen} \times 2 \text{ ounces}}{36 \times 6 \text{ ounces}} = \frac{66 \times 2 \text{ ounces}}{36 \times 6 \text{ ounces}} = \frac{132 \text{ ounces}}{216 \text{ ounces}} = .6111$$

As you can see from these examples, when the yield of a recipe is increased, the RCF is always greater than 1, and when the yield of a recipe is decreased, the RCF is always less than 1.

Next, we will discuss how RCF is used to convert recipes.

Applying the Recipe Conversion Factor

red pepper coulis

Yield: 1 quart

> 3 pounds red peppers, chopped
>
> 4 ounces onion, chopped
>
> 2 garlic cloves, minced
>
> 1/4 jalapeño, minced
>
> 2 tablespoons olive oil
>
> 1 1/2 pints chicken stock
>
> 2 tablespoons balsamic vinegar
>
> 1/2 teaspoon salt
>
> Pinch black pepper

Change the yield of the red pepper coulis to 1 1/2 gallons. Calculate the RCF:

$$\frac{New}{Old} = \frac{1\ 1/2\ gallons}{1\ quart} = \frac{6\ \cancel{quarts}}{1\ \cancel{quart}} = 6$$

Use the RCF, which is 6, to adjust the ingredients in the original recipe to yield the new desired amount. To accomplish this, multiply each ingredient by the RCF.

RED PEPPER COULIS		
ORIGINAL (OLD) RECIPE INGREDIENTS:	RCF	NEW RECIPE INGREDIENTS:
3 pounds red peppers, chopped	× 6	18 pounds
4 ounces onion, chopped	× 6	24 ounces
2 garlic cloves, minced	× 6	12 cloves
1/4 jalapeño, minced	× 6	1 1/2 each
2 tablespoons olive oil	× 6	6 tablespoons
1 1/2 pints chicken stock	× 6	9 pints
2 tablespoons balsamic vinegar	× 6	12 tablespoons
1/2 teaspoon salt	× 6	3 teaspoons
Pinch black pepper	× 6	6 pinches

Making the New Recipe Easier to Measure

AFTER CALCULATING THE RCF and the new ingredient quantities, apply your knowledge of ingredients and how they affect taste and texture, as well as your knowledge of units of measure, to adjust the new ingredient quantities to more reasonable measures.

RED PEPPER COULIS

ORIGINAL (OLD) RECIPE INGREDIENTS	RCF	NEW RECIPE INGREDIENTS	ADJUSTED INGREDIENTS
3 pounds red peppers, chopped	× 6	18 pounds	18 pounds
For the red peppers, 18 pounds is an acceptable measurement.			
4 ounces onion, chopped	× 6	24 ounces	1 1/2 pounds or 1 pound 8 ounces
For the onions, we could use 24 ounces or convert it to pounds.			
2 garlic cloves, minced	× 6	12 cloves	12 cloves
For the garlic cloves, 12 cloves is an acceptable measurement.			
1/4 jalapeño, minced	× 6	1 1/2 each	1 1/2 each
For the jalapeno, 1 1/2 each is fine. However, see "danger" note on page 124 for further discussion.			
2 tablespoons olive oil	× 6	6 tablespoons	6 tablespoons or 1/4 cup plus 2 tablespoons
For the olive oil, 6 tablespoons is fine. However, you may want to convert it to a mixed measure—in this case, cups and tablespoons.			
1 1/2 pints chicken stock	× 6	9 pints	1 gallon plus 1 pint
For the chicken stock, 9 pints is not an especially reasonable measure. Converting it to gallons makes sense.			
2 tablespoons balsamic vinegar	× 6	12 tablespoons	3/4 cup
For balsamic vinegar, 12 tablespoons converts nicely to 3/4 cup.			
1/2 teaspoon salt	× 6	3 teaspoons	1 tablespoon
For salt, 3 teaspoons converts nicely to 1 tablespoon. However, see "danger" note on page 124 for further discussion.			
Pinch black pepper	× 6	6 pinches	1/2 teaspoon
For black pepper, a pinch is generally considered something less than 1/8 teaspoon. So, if you multiply 1/8 by 6, it becomes 6/8 or 3/4 teaspoon. Since a pinch is less than 1/8 teaspoon, though, you should probably start with 1/2 teaspoon and add to taste.			

cider sauce

Yield: 1 quart

1 quart apple cider

3 fluid ounces cider vinegar

1 pint fond de veau lié

1/4 teaspoon salt

1/4 teaspoon ground black pepper

1 1/2 pounds Granny Smith apples

Danger

When changing a recipe to yield less there is a temptation to divide. Keep in mind that you must ALWAYS multiply by the RCF. (Multiplying by .25 is the same as dividing by 4!)

If you would like to make just 1 cup of this sauce, you need to calculate the recipe conversion factor.

$$\frac{\text{New}}{\text{Old}} = \frac{1\,\text{cup}}{1\,\text{quart}} = \frac{1\,\cancel{\text{cup}}}{4\,\cancel{\text{cups}}} = .25$$

ORIGINAL (OLD) RECIPE INGREDIENTS	RCF	NEW RECIPE INGREDIENTS
1 quart apple cider	× .25	.25 quart
3 fluid ounces cider vinegar	× .25	.75 fluid ounce
1 pint fond de veau lié	× .25	.25 pint
1/4 teaspoon salt	× .25	.0625 teaspoon
1/4 teaspoon ground black pepper	× .25	.0625 teaspoon
1 1/2 pounds Granny Smith apples	× .25	.375 pound

CIDER SAUCE

ORIGINAL (OLD) RECIPE INGREDIENTS	RCF	NEW RECIPE INGREDIENTS	ADJUSTED INGREDIENTS
1 quart apple cider	× .25	.25 quart	1 cup

For the apple cider, 1/4 quart converts nicely to 1 cup.

ORIGINAL (OLD) RECIPE INGREDIENTS	RCF	NEW RECIPE INGREDIENTS	ADJUSTED INGREDIENTS
3 fluid ounces cider vinegar	× .25	.75 fluid ounce	1 tablespoon plus 1 1/2 teaspoons

For the cider vinegar, converting to tablespoons makes the most sense. Since 1 tablespoon is .5 ounce, .75 ounce would be 1 1/2 tablespoons. It is difficult to measure 1/2 tablespoon. Half of 1 tablespoon is 1 1/2 teaspoons. So the most accurate way to measure the cider vinegar is 1 tablespoon plus 1 1/2 teaspoons.

ORIGINAL (OLD) RECIPE INGREDIENTS	RCF	NEW RECIPE INGREDIENTS	ADJUSTED INGREDIENTS
1 pint fond de veau lié	× .25	.25 pint	1/2 cup

For the fond de veau lié, 1/4 pint converts nicely to 1/2 cup.

ORIGINAL (OLD) RECIPE INGREDIENTS	RCF	NEW RECIPE INGREDIENTS	ADJUSTED INGREDIENTS
1/4 teaspoon salt	× .25	.0625 teaspoon	pinch

For the salt, .0625 teaspoons is 1/16 of a teaspoon—too small to measure. Anything less than 1/8 (.125 teaspoon) is a pinch.

ORIGINAL (OLD) RECIPE INGREDIENTS	RCF	NEW RECIPE INGREDIENTS	ADJUSTED INGREDIENTS
1/4 teaspoon ground black pepper	× .25	.0625 teaspoon	pinch

For the pepper, .0625 teaspoons is 1/16 of a teaspoon—too small to measure. Anything less than 1/8 teaspoon (.125 teaspoon) is a pinch.

ORIGINAL (OLD) RECIPE INGREDIENTS	RCF	NEW RECIPE INGREDIENTS	ADJUSTED INGREDIENTS
1/2 pounds Granny Smith apples	× .25	.375 pound	6 ounces

For the apples, .375 pounds is okay, or you could change it to ounces—.375 pounds is 6 ounces.

When adjusting the recipe at the end of this process, be careful not to alter individual amounts so much that the outcome will be affected. Words such as *heaping* and *scant* may help to describe amounts that are not quite whole measures; heaping and scant measures are especially appropriate for recipes that are being developed for the home cook.

HEAPING AND SCANT

Heaping describes a measure that is slightly fuller than level. For example, 1.096 tablespoon converts nicely to a heaping tablespoon. *Scant* describes a measure that is slightly less full than level. For example, .98 teaspoon converts nicely to a scant teaspoon.

When scaling recipes up or down for use in a professional kitchen, however, and especially when creating a recipe for standard use, terms such as *heaping* and *scant* should not be used. These terms are not exact measures and cannot be used effectively for costing recipes or maintaining inventory. For this situation, the new ingredient amounts should be rounded to the nearest measurable number. If the recipe is being scaled for the creation of a standard recipe, the newly calculated recipe should be tested and any necessary alterations made.

It is important to remember that you should always go back to the original recipe to convert a recipe again. For instance, if you wanted to make 1 gallon of the cider sauce, you should convert from the original recipe, not from the adjusted recipe.

Remember that changing a recipe's yield also affects the mixing time, pan size, cooking temperature, and cooking time. These cannot be adjusted by the recipe conversion factor. For instance, if you double an oatmeal raisin cookie recipe that bakes at 375°F, it would not be smart to double the temperature and bake the cookies at 750°F. As you become more familiar with the science and art of food preparation, you will learn how to handle these situations in each case.

Conclusion

RECIPE CONVERSION is a common occurrence in a foodservice operation. Whether you are converting some recipes so that you may give them to customers or print them in cooking magazines, or changing recipes to serve at a very large banquet you will find that this approach saves time and maintains the integrity of the recipe.

Chapter in Review

1. A recipe for corn chowder makes one hundred and fifty 6-ounce servings. You will be making forty 8-ounce servings. What would the recipe conversion factor be?

2. A recipe for potato salad yields 5 gallons of potato salad. The recipe calls for 2 quarts of sour cream. How many cups of sour cream should you add if you want to make 1 1/2 gallons of potato salad?

3. A recipe for red fruit compote makes 10 servings of 3/4 cup each. If you would like to make 40 servings of 1/2 cup each, what would be the recipe conversion factor?

4. A recipe for chilled red plum soup makes 1 gallon of soup. The recipe calls for 2 tablespoons of lemon juice. How many cups of lemon juice should you use if you want to make 200 portions of the soup and each portion is to be 3/4 cup?

5. A recipe for tomato sauce makes 2 quarts and calls for 1 pint of tomato purée. If you need to make 100 half-cup servings, how many quarts of tomato puree should you use?

6. You are making a gratin of fresh fruits. The recipe makes 8 servings. You need to make 15 servings. What would the recipe conversion factor be?

7. A recipe for baker's cheese filling makes 4 1/2 pounds of filling. The recipe calls for 2 1/2 pounds cheese, 1/4 ounce vanilla, and other ingredients. You are making cheese-filled danish. Each danish is to contain 1 3/4 ounces of the cheese filling. If you are making 25 dozen danish, how much of the cheese and how much of the vanilla should you use?

8. Explain why the recipe conversion factor is always greater than 1 when increasing a recipe and always less than 1 when decreasing a recipe.

9. What is the major benefit to using the recipe conversion factor?

10. The following recipe for fire and ice piquant onions makes eight 1/3-cup servings. Adjust the recipe to make 3 gallons of fire and ice piquant onions.

FIRE AND ICE PIQUANT ONIONS		
	YIELD: 8 1/3-CUP SERVINGS	**ADJUSTED YIELD: 3 GALLONS**
INGREDIENTS	**STANDARD QUANTITY**	**ADJUSTED QUANTITY**
Red onions	2 ea	
Tomatoes	1.25 pounds	
Bell peppers	1 ea	
Cider vinegar	3/4 cup	
Water	1/4 cup	
Celery seed	1 1/2 tsp	
Mustard seed	2 tsp	
Red pepper	1/2 tsp	
Salt	1 tsp	
Sugar	1 tbsp	
Black pepper	1/3 tsp	

11. Adjust the following recipe as indicated.

ORANGE HONEY BUTTER

INGREDIENTS	YIELD: 50 SERVINGS STANDARD QUANTITY	ADJUSTED YIELD: 8 SERVINGS ADJUSTED QUANTITY
Butter	3 pounds	
Honey	8 pounds	
Brown sugar	2 pounds	
Cinnamon	1 1/2 tsp	
Orange brandy	3/4 cup	
Lemon peel	2 tbsp	
Orange peel	1/3 cup	
Pecans, chopped	1/3 cup	

12. A recipe for crème brûlée makes twenty-eight 8-ounce servings. The recipe calls for 4 quarts of heavy cream. If you want to make ninety-seven 8-ounce servings, how much heavy cream do you need?

13. You need to make spaghetti sauce for 380 people. Your current recipe calls for 20 cups of tomatoes, 4 tablespoons of chopped garlic, 1 cup of diced onions, and 1 1/2 pounds of ground beef. Your recipe makes enough sauce to serve 40 people. How much of each ingredient do you need to make enough for 380 people?

14. A recipe for stir-fried vegetables makes fifteen 4-ounce servings. You will be making eighty 3-ounce servings. What is the recipe conversion factor?

15. A lemonade recipe that makes eight 10-ounce servings calls for 3 1/3 cups of fresh lemon juice, 5 2/3 cups of water, and 8 ounces of granulated sugar. You need to make one hundred 4-ounce servings for a party that you are catering. How many pounds of lemons do you need to purchase if the yield percentage is 45 percent and each lemon weighs 5 ounces?

16. A recipe for cheesecake makes 2 cakes with 16 servings each. If you want to make 80 servings, what would the recipe conversion factor be?

17. A recipe for soup makes 1 1/2 gallons and calls for 15 ounces of fresh shucked corn.

   A. If you want to make ten 6-ounce servings, how many ounces of fresh shucked corn should you use?

   B. You want to make 6 gallons of soup. If 1 ear of corn yields 8 ounces of shucked corn, how many ears of corn should you order?

18. You have been asked to prepare Caesar salad for 120 people. The recipe you are working with serves 8 people.

   A. What is the recipe conversion factor?

   B. If the original recipe called for 1 1/2 cups of oil, how many gallons of oil should you use to make the 120 servings?

19. A recipe for margaritas calls for 10 limes for 8 servings. You will be making margaritas for 5 people. How many limes should you use?

20. Additional Challenge: You have a recipe for asparagus soup that yields ten 6-ounce servings of soup. The recipe calls for 1 teaspoon of lemon zest and 2 ounces of diced onions (among other ingredients).

    A. You would like to use this recipe for a party you are catering for 175 guests. Each guest will receive a 5-ounce serving. How much lemon zest and diced onions should you use for the soup for this party?

    B. How many pounds of lemons should you order for this party if each lemon yields 2 teaspoons of zest, and each lemon weighs approximately 3.5 ounces?

    C. How many pounds of onions should you order for this party if onions have an 87 percent yield?

CHAPTER **13**

goals

- Calculate ingredient quantities for a given ratio when the total to be made is known

- Calculate the quantities for the remaining ingredients in a given ratio when the quantity of one of the ingredient is known

Kitchen Ratios

You are working dinner service and need to make additional vinaigrette. There is 1 liter (33.8 fluid ounces) of olive oil to make the vinaigrette. How much vinegar do you add to the oil to have the correct ratio for vinaigrette (3 parts oil to 1 part vinegar)?

Using Ratios

THE USE OF RATIOS is an important part of food preparation. A ratio can be thought of as a mathematically formulated recipe. Unlike recipes, which deal in specific measured amounts, terms for ratios, such as "equal parts," give a specific relation between the ingredients.

An example would be the ratio for vinaigrette: 3 parts oil, 1 part vinegar. If this ratio were 1 part to 1 part, you would use the same amounts of oil and vinegar. Since there are three parts of oil and 1 part of vinegar, there will be three times more oil in the vinaigrette than vinegar.

By contrast, here is a recipe for tomato salsa:

1 pound tomato concassé
3 ounces red onion, minced
1/2 ounce jalapeño, minced
3 tablespoons chopped cilantro
3 tablespoons lime juice
1 teaspoon salt
1/2 teaspoon crushed black peppercorns

In this recipe there are four different measurements used to describe the ingredient quantities: pounds, ounces, tablespoons, and teaspoons. Unlike the vinaigrette ratio, the tomato salsa recipe gives unrelated quantities.

Many recipes can be converted into ratios. Remembering key ratios instead of large and sometimes complicated recipes can help to simplify the job of the chef. The use of ratios allows a chef to recall a large number of recipes by remembering one basic relationship (the ratio), rather than memorizing each individual recipe; the recipe can then be customized by adding seasonings and other ingredients.

A ratio is described in parts. The parts are all of the same unit of measure. It is up to the individual using the ratio to determine what that unit of measure will be. For example, tablespoons or quarts can be used to make vinaigrette using the ratio, and the resulting vinaigrettes will vary only in quantity. However, the units of measurement must be the same. Tablespoons cannot be used for one part of the ratio and quarts for the other.

The ratios that will be discussed involve a single unit of measure. These ratios can be applied using weight measurements or volume measurements, depending on the ingredients.

Ratios are sometimes given as percentages. In those cases, the percentage should be multiplied by the whole to determine the proper amount for the ingredient.

One basic ratio used in the kitchen is the ratio for mirepoix (see Figure 13.1). Mirepoix is a combination of chopped aromatic vegetables used to flavor stocks, soups, braises, and stews.

FIGURE 13.1. The standard mirepoix ratio is shown here.

COMMON KITCHEN RATIOS

MIREPOIX

Carrots	25%
Celery	25%
Onions	50%

Ratios discussed in this chapter will be given in parts.

MIREPOIX

Carrots	1 part
Celery	1 part
Onions	2 parts

Other common kitchen ratios in standard and percentage form:

White Rice	or	White Rice
1 part rice		33 1/3% rice
2 parts liquid		66 2/3% liquid

Brown Rice	or	Brown Rice
1 part rice		28.5% rice
2.5 parts liquid		71.5% liquid

Vinaigrette	or	Vinaigrette
3 parts oil		75% oil
1 part vinegar		25% vinegar

The ratios listed above will work with weight measures or with volume measures. For example, to make rice, you could use 1 cup of rice and 2 cups of water. Or you could make rice with 1 pound of rice and 2 pounds of water. However, this is not universally true for ratios. The only reason the ratios listed above may be measured in volume or in weight is because any weight-to-volume difference between the ingredients listed in these

Many chefs think of short recipes as ratios. For example:

CHICKEN STOCK
Yield: 1 gallon
8 lb chicken bones
6 qt water
1 lb mirepoix
1 standard sachet d'épices

While it is not wrong to think of this as a ratio, it is not the type of ratio being referred to when discussing the math used to calculate ingredient quantities from ratios. This type of ratio is better referred to as a *formula*. This formula is really a short recipe, because the ingredients do not have equal units of measure

ratios is negligible. See the sidebar for some special cases in which the volume-to-weight differences are important.

Calculating Ingredient Quantities with Ratios

THERE ARE TWO SITUATIONS that may occur in dealing with kitchen ratios: when the total amount to be made is known or is unknown.

When the Total Amount to Be Made Is *Known*

Here are the steps for determining ingredient quantities when the total amount that needs to be made is known.

1. Determine the total quantity to be made.

2. Find the total number of parts in the ratio.

3. Find the amount per part for this situation by dividing the total quantity to be made by the total number of parts.

4. Find the amount of each ingredient by multiplying each ingredient by the amount per part.

Example: You will be making 10 gallons of soup. For every 1 gallon of soup, you need 1 pound of mirepoix. How many pounds of each of the ingredients should be used in the mirepoix for this soup?

1. Determine the total quantity to be made.

    If you were making 10 gallons of soup and need 1 pound of mirepoix for each gallon of soup, you would need a total of 10 pounds of mirepoix. (10 × 1#=10#)

2. Find the total number of parts in the ratio.

> Mirepoix
>
> 2 parts onions
>
> 1 part celery
>
> +<u>1 part carrots</u>
>
> 4 parts total

3. Find the amount per part for this situation by dividing the total quantity to be made by the total number of parts.

> Determine the quantity (in this case the weight) of each part. To do this, divide the total weight (10#) by the number of parts there are in the ratio. For mirepoix there are 4 parts, so divide 10 pounds by 4 parts (10 pounds ÷ 4 parts = 2.5 pounds). Each part in our ratio will weigh 2.5 pounds.

4. Find the amount of each ingredient by multiplying each ingredient by the amount per part.

> The final step in this procedure is to take the weight or quantity in each part (the 2.5#) and multiply that amount by the number of parts for a particular ingredient.

> Onions 2 parts × 2.5# = 5 #
>
> Celery   1 part × 2.5# = 2.5#
>
> Carrots <u>1 part × 2.5# = 2.5#</u>
>
>   Total = 10 #

> **Finding the total is a good way to check your work.**

When the Total to Be Made is *Unknown*

Sometimes you do not know the total amount that you will be making. What you do know is the amount of one of the ingredients in the ratio. For instance, the introduction to this chapter presents a situation in which you know the amount of oil that you have but need to determine the amount of vinegar to add to it to make vinaigrette.

Here are the steps for determining ingredient quantities when the total to be made is unknown:

1. Find the amount per part for this situation by dividing the amount that you know by the number of parts it represents.

2. Multiply the amount per part by the number of parts for each of the remaining ingredients.

Example: You are working the dinner service and need to make additional vinaigrette for tonight. There is 1 liter (33.8 fluid ounces) of olive oil to make the vinaigrette. How much vinegar do you add to the oil to have the correct ratio for vinaigrette (3 parts oil to 1 part vinegar)?

1. Find the amount per part for this situation by dividing the amount that you know by the number of parts that it represents.

    Divide the 33.8 ounces of olive oil by the number of parts the oil represents in the ratio.

    Ratio for Vinaigrette

    3 parts oil

    1 part vinegar

    33.8 ounces ÷ 3 parts = 11.266 ounces per part

2. Multiply the amount per part by the number of parts for each of the remaining ingredients.

    Oil = 33.8 ounces (given)

    Vinegar = 11.266 ounces × 1 part = 11.266 ounces

According to the calculations, 11.266 ounces of vinegar should be added to the 33.8 ounces of olive oil to make vinaigrette. The total amount of vinaigrette that will be made is 45.066 ounces.

Example: Your chef hands you 7 pounds of chopped onions and asks you to make mirepoix using those onions. How many pounds of celery and how many pounds of carrots should be added to the onions to make the mirepoix? How many pounds of mirepoix will there be in total?

1. Find the amount per part for this situation by dividing the amount that you know by the number of parts that it represents.

Divide the 7 pounds of onions by the number of parts the onions represent in the ratio for mirepoix.

Mirepoix Ratio

2 parts onions

1 part celery

1 part carrots

7 pounds ÷ 2 parts = 3.5 pounds per part

2. Multiply the amount per part by the number of parts for each of the remaining ingredients.

Multiply the remaining ingredients by the amount per part.

Onions   2 parts = 7# (given)

Celery   1 part × 3.5# = 3.5#

Carrots   1 part × 3.5# = 3.5#

According to the calculations, 3.5 pounds of celery and 3.5 pounds of carrots should be added to the 7 pounds of onions to make mirepoix. There will be 14 pounds of mirepoix in total.

Conclusion

RATIOS CAN BE USED to simplify a number of basic recipes. New recipes can be built on the foundation of proven, basic ratios. Creative approaches by adding different seasonings and flavorings to old ratios will create exciting recipes that are unique.

Chapter in Review

Use the ratios on the previous page for any ratios that you might need.

1. You need 2 1/2 gallons of vinaigrette for a party that you are catering. How many quarts of oil and vinegar do you need?

2. You are going to serve vinaigrette to 62 people at a luncheon. Each person will be served 2 tablespoons of dressing on the side. How many ounces of oil and how many ounces of vinegar do you need to make the vinaigrette for this luncheon?

3. You have 5 pounds 10 ounces of butter. How many pounds of flour and sugar do you need to add to it to make cookie dough?

4. You will be serving 325 people brown rice. You know that 1 ounce of raw rice, when cooked, will produce 1 portion. How many pounds of rice and how many gallons of liquid will you need to make the brown rice for this function?

5. A. Calculate the amount of oil and vinegar you would use to make 7 gallons of basic vinaigrette dressing.

B. How many ounces of oil would be in each serving of dressing if each portion contained 2 ounces?

6. You have 7 pounds 12 ounces of onions. You want to make mirepoix with the onions. How many pounds of carrots and how many pounds of celery must you use in order to use all the onions?

7. A. A basic chocolate sauce is produced with 6 parts chocolate, 5 parts heavy cream, and 1 part butter. If we were to make a chocolate sauce using 17.5 ounces of heavy cream, how much chocolate would we have to use?

B. Using the basic chocolate sauce ratio, compute how many ounces of each ingredient you should use if you want to make 40 portions of chocolate sauce and each portion is to be 1 1/2 ounces.

8. The standard ratio for dauphine potatoes is 1 part pâte à choux to 2 parts peeled chef potatoes. How many pounds of chef potatoes do you need to order if you want to produce one hundred and fifty 4 1/2-ounce portions and potatoes have a 78.2 percent yield?

9. If you need to make two hundred and forty 3-ounce tart shells, how many pounds of each ingredient should you use if you use the standard ratio for piecrust?

10. A special dough ratio is as follows:

2 1/2 parts flour

2 parts butter

1 part liquid

You have 3 pounds 12 ounces of flour. How many pounds of each of the other ingredients should you add to make this dough?

11. There is a banquet for 380 people and you need prebaked pie shells for toffee caramel mousse pie. Using the standard ratio for pie crust, compute how much of each ingredient you should use if 1 pie will serve 8 people and requires 10 ounces of pie dough.

12. A. The basic ratio for custard is as follows:

4 parts milk

2 parts egg

1 part sugar

If you want to make 14 pounds 6 ounces of custard, how many ounces of each ingredient should you use?

B. You need to make custard and are going to use 2 gallons of milk. How many ounces of the other ingredients should you add to the milk to make the custard?

Use the following ratio for problems 14–16.

Linda and Julie's Special Fruit Salad Ratio

4 parts diced watermelon

3 parts sliced banana

3 1/2 parts diced cantaloupe

2 1/2 parts diced honeydew

1/4 part shredded coconut

14. You would like to make enough to serve 40 people 4 ounces of fruit salad each. How many bananas will you need to order to make this delicious summer dessert?

15. If you have 9 1/2# of cleaned watermelon, how many pounds of honeydew will you need to order to make this fruit salad?

16. If you would like to make 8 1/2# of fruit salad, how much of each ingredient do you need to have cleaned?

CHAPTER 14

Metric Measures

You are working the line in a French restaurant. While you are assembling your mise en place, the chef asks you to get him 100 grams of butter. You go into the walk-in and grab 3 cases of butter because 100 grams sure sounds like a lot. The chef sees you coming out of the walk-in and starts laughing. What went wrong?

The next day the sous chef wants you to gather the mise en place for a recipe. He gives you the standard recipe that is used in the restaurant, but all the measurements are in metric amounts.

You may come across situations involving metric measures whether you are working in the United States or abroad. Many goods produced in other countries are sold in metric amounts, and wines and spirits come bottled in metric units. This chapter explains the metric system and its relationship to the U.S. standard system as used in the foodservice industry (see Figure 14.1).

FIGURE 14.1 **Metric measurements are important to know in relation to their U.S. equivalents.**

goals

- Identify the areas in foodservice where the metric system may be used

- Apply the equivalents for the metric system and the U.S. standard system as they will be used in the kitchen

- Convert recipes into standard U.S. or metric measure

- Calculate the number of U.S. standard-measure servings of wine or spirits that can be poured from a quantity given in metric measure

- Calculate the liquor cost percentage given the cost per drink and the selling price

Uses and Advantages of Metric Measures

THERE ARE A NUMBER of kitchen situations in which knowledge of the metric system is important. A few examples are:

- Working in a country where the measurement of choice is metric
- Ordering ingredients from overseas that are packaged in metric amounts
- Calculating nutritional information
- Determining the cost per drink or the number of servings that a given quantity of wine or spirits will serve
- Using recipes from countries where ingredients are listed in metric quantities

There are many advantages to using metric measures.

- It is an internationally recognized system of measure.
- The system is based on the number 10, which makes calculating easier.
- Recording very small measures is easier and therefore more accurate.

The Metric System

THERE ARE MANY METRIC MEASURES. The conversions used most often in food-service are:

WEIGHT (MASS)	LIQUID (VOLUME)
1 gram = 1000 milligrams	1 liter = 33.8 fluid ounces
1000 grams = 1 kilogram	1000 milliliters = 1 liter
1 ounce = 28.35 grams	1000 liters = 1 kiloliter
1 kilogram = 2.21 lbs.	

It is imperative to know these conversions as thoroughly as the U.S. standard measures conversions (*see* Chapter 2).

The following figure gives the standard abbreviations for the metric measurements that are used in the foodservice industry.

METRIC BASE UNIT ABBREVIATIONS		OTHER COMMON METRIC ABBREVIATIONS	
liter	L	milliliter	mL
gram	g	kilogram	kg

The metric system is a system based on the number 10. The following figure lists the common metric prefixes and their relationship to the base unit—grams, liters, or meters.

METRIC PREFIX
kilo- = 1000 base units
deka- =10 base units
deci- =.1 base unit
centi- =.01 base unit
milli- =.001 base unit

BASE UNIT	KILO-	DEKA-	DECI-	CENTI-	MILLI-
gram	kilogram	dekagram	decigram	centigram	milligram
liter	kiloliter	dekaliter	deciliter	centiliter	milliliter

FIGURE 14.2. **The smallest commonly used metric unit of weight is the gram. It is much smaller than the smallest commonly used unit of weight in the United States, the ounce. A *gram* of chocolate is on the *left* and the *ounce* is on the *right*.**

When converting between U.S. standard measures and metric measures, it is easiest to use the bridge method (*see* Chapter 3).

Example: How many ounces are in 100 grams of butter?

$$\frac{100 \cancel{g}}{1} \times \frac{1 \text{ oz}}{28.34 \cancel{g}} = \frac{100}{28.35} = 3.5273 \text{ oz}$$

Example: A gallon of water is equivalent to how many liters?

$$\frac{1 \cancel{\text{gallon}}}{1} \times \frac{128 \text{ fl oz}}{1 \cancel{\text{gallon}}} = \frac{128 \cancel{\text{fl oz}}}{1} \times \frac{1 \text{ L}}{33.8 \cancel{\text{fl oz}}} = \frac{128}{33.8} = 3.7869 \text{ L}$$

The Math of Wines

MOST ESTATE WINES are bottled in the following standard bottle sizes.

SIZE	ML PER BOTTLE	BOTTLES PER CASE	ML PER CASE
1/2 bottle (split)	187.5 mL	48	9,000
1/2 bottle	375 mL	24	9,000
Bottle	750 mL	12	9,000
Magnum	1500 mL	6	9,000

There are always 9,000 milliliters or 9 liters of wine in a case no matter the size of the bottles.

The Math of Spirits

SPIRITS SUCH AS rum, gin, and vodka are, like wines, packed by milliliters or liters. The common bottle sizes in the foodservice industry are:

SIZE	NUMBER PER CASE	ML PER CASE
750-mL bottles	12 to a case	9,000
1 liter bottles	12 to a case	12,000

Example: How many fluid ounces are in 750 milliliters?

$$\frac{750 \text{ mL}}{1} \times \frac{1 \text{ L}}{1000 \text{ mL}} = \frac{750 \text{ L}}{1000} = \frac{.75 \text{ L}}{1} = \frac{33.8 \text{ fl oz}}{1 \text{ L}} = 25.35 \text{ fl oz}$$

Example: How many 5–fl-oz drinks can be poured from a case of wine?

$$\frac{9 \text{ L}}{1} \times \frac{33.8 \text{ fl oz}}{1 \text{ L}} = \frac{304.2 \text{ fl oz}}{1} \times \frac{1 \text{ drink}}{5 \text{ fl oz}} = \frac{304.2}{5} = 61.04 \text{ or } 61 \text{ drinks}$$

Liquor Cost Percentage

THE LIQUOR COST PERCENTAGE (LC%) is similar to the food cost percentage, which was discussed in Chapter 9. Food cost percentage and liquor cost percentage are the percentage of the selling price that pays for the food or liquor. When the food cost percentage is 30 percent, the amount of the selling price that goes for food cost is 30 percent. When the liquor cost percentage is 14 percent, the amount of the selling price for a drink that pays for the liquor is 14 percent.

> **Hint**
>
> It is very important to make sure that the units are the same for the cost and the sales before you divide.

$$\text{Liquor Cost Percentage} = \frac{\text{Liquor Cost}}{\text{Liquor Sales}}$$

Example: A case of liter bottles of vodka costs $180.95. The case should generate $1389.62 in sales. What is the liquor cost percentage?

$$\text{Liquor Cost Percentage} = \frac{\text{Liquor Cost}}{\text{Liquor Sales}} = \frac{\$180.95}{\$1389.62} = 13.02\%$$

Example: A liter bottle of vodka costs $15.08. How many 1 1/2-ounce drinks can be poured from the bottle? If $4.50 is charged for the 1 1/2-ounce drink, what is the liquor cost percentage?

$$1 \text{ L} = \frac{33.8 \text{ fl oz}}{1} \times \frac{1 \text{ drink}}{1 \text{ 1/2 fl oz}} = \frac{33.8}{1.5} = 22.53333 \text{ or } 22 \text{ drinks}$$

22 drinks × $4.50 per drink = $99.00

$$\text{Liquor Cost Percentage} = \frac{\text{Liquor Cost}}{\text{Liquor Sales}} = \frac{\$15.08}{\$99.00} = 15.23\%$$

Conclusion

BEING FAMILIAR with metric units of measure that are commonly used in the kitchen is imperative for success in the foodservice industry. Without this knowledge, many costly calculation and ordering errors will be made. The math covered in this chapter will help you to prevent this from happening.

Chapter in Review

1. How many grams are in 1 pound?

2. If a recipe calls for 6 cups of peeled diced apples, how many grams of apples would you need?

3. You have 2.5 kilograms of honey. How many quarts of honey are in the 2.5 kilograms?

4. How many ounces are in 1 kilogram?

5. Your restaurant is hosting a New Year's Eve party for 225 people. Each person is to receive two 2.5-ounce glasses of complimentary champagne. You will also need 2 bottles of champagne to give away as door prizes. How many cases must you buy if you purchase 750-mL bottles that are packed 12 to a case?

6. Your purveyor found some authentic olive oil, but it is sold in 750-mL bottles. If you need to make vinaigrette dressing for 200 guests and each person will receive 1.5 ounces of dressing, how many bottles of olive oil will you need? (3 parts oil to 1 part vinegar)

7. You purchase 1 kilogram of honey. If 1 cup of honey weighs .75#, how many cups of honey do you have?

8. You purchase 500 mL of vanilla extract. How many teaspoons of vanilla do you have?

9. How many pounds of flour are in an 11-kilogram bag of flour?

10. You are making 10 cakes. Each cake will contain 5 ounces of ground hazelnuts. How many kilograms of hazelnuts will you need?

11. If 1 chicken weighs 5 pounds, how many kilograms do 3 chickens weigh?

12. You are going to cater a wedding for 350 people. Each guest will have two 5-ounce glasses of wine. The wine is purchased at $90.00 per case with 9 liters per case.

  A. How many cases will you need?

  B. How much will it cost per guest?

13. If a recipe calls for 1140 grams of chocolate, how many pounds do you need to order?

14. How many 4-oz drinks can be poured from a 750 mL bottle of wine?

15. If we purchase liter bottles of whiskey, how many 1 1/4-oz drinks can be poured from one bottle?

16. The house purchases 3 cases of gin in liter bottles for $575.28. If the house pours 1 3/4-oz drinks, how many drinks can be poured from the 3 cases? How much will each drink cost?

17. A drink recipe for a black Russian calls for 1 3/4 oz of vodka and 3/4 oz of Kahlúa. How much vodka and how much Kahlúa should you use for a drink totaling 3.25 ounces?

18. If it takes 3/4 oz of cream to produce a 3-oz cocktail, how much will be required to produce a 5-oz cocktail?

19. A measured liter bottle of a spirit has only 430 mL remaining. What percentage of the bottle does this represent? If the bottle cost is $18.50, what is the value of the spirits that remain?

20. A case of 750-mL bottles of tequila costs $178.50. If this same tequila is packed in liter bottles, the case will cost $228.00. Which case is the better buy?

21. A case of liter bottles of spirits costs $87.50. How many 1 3/4-oz drinks will the case yield? How much money will the case generate if we sell each drink for $2.50? The cost will be what percentage of sales?

CHAPTER 15

Review

The following is a selection of problems designed to assist you in determining your understanding of the material covered in this text. At this point you should be able to solve these problems and problems like these successfully. If you struggle with any of these problems review the chapter(s) in which the math is covered (*chapter number is noted in parenthesis*).

1. You need to use 1134 grams of rice.

A. How many cups of rice should you use if 1 cup of rice weighs 8 ounces? (*chapter 14*)

B. If the ratio of rice to stock is 1 part rice to 3 parts stock how many cups of stock should you use? (*chapter 13*)

2. A recipe for soup makes 5 gallons and calls for 2 cups of tomato juice. You want to make thirty 6-ounce portions. How many cups of tomato juice should you use? (1 cup of soup is 8 ounces) (*chapter 13*)

3. A restaurant orders 5 cases (750-mL bottles) of red wine in the beginning of the week. They pay $297 for the 5 cases. At the end of the week there were 18 bottles left. Answer the following questions:

   A. What percent of the cases were sold?

   B. If each bottle sold for $21.50, what would the Liquor Cost Percent be?

   C. If we decided to sell the remaining bottles by the glass how many glasses could be poured if each glass held 6 ounces? (*chapter 14*)

4. You are making apple pies. Each pie needs 2 pounds 9 ounces of cleaned apples. How many apple pies can be made from 20 pounds of apples if the yield is 82%? (*chapter 10*)

5. How many heads of lettuce must be purchased to serve 110 people each a 6-ounce portion if the yield on lettuce is 72% and each head weighs 2 1/4 pounds? (*chapter 10*)

6. In what instance is the edible portion cost equal to the as-purchased cost? (*chapter 8*)

7. Complete the *Roasted Snapper with Tropical Tubers* food cost form. (*chapter 9*)

8. How many pounds of Yucca should you order to make the *Roasted Snapper with Tropical Tubers?* (*chapter 10*)

9. How many bunches of Oregano should you order if you want to make 300 portions of the *Roasted Snapper with Tropical Tubers?* (*chapter 10*)

For questions 10 and 11 use the following ratio:

Winter Fruit Salad
3 parts apples
2 parts pears
1 1/2 parts oranges
1/2 part mixed dried fruit

10. You would like to make fifty five, 3-ounce portions of Winter Fruit Salad. How many pounds of each ingredient should you order? The yield percent for apples is 85%, pears is 76.6% and oranges is 62.5%. (*chapter 13*)

11. If you have ordered 6 pounds of pears how many pounds of apples should you order to make this Winter Fruit Salad? (*chapter 13*)

12. We are serving 2 chocolate dipped strawberries to each of the 60 guests. The yield percent for large strawberries is 87%. We purchase strawberries by the pint and each pint contains 13 berries and weighs approximately 11 ounces. Strawberries cost $1.75 per pint. How many quarts of strawberries should we purchase and how much will each serving cost? (*chapter 11*)

Menu Item _____ **Roasted Snapper with Tropical Tubers** _____ Date _____
Number of Portions _____ **30 Servings** _____ Size _____
Cost per Portion _____ Selling price _____ Food Cost % ___ **30%** ___

Ingredients	Recipe Quantity (EP)			Cost			Total Cost
	Weight	Volume	Count	APC/Unit	Yield %	EPC/Unit	
Red Snapper	11# 3 oz			$3.89/#	100%		
Key Limes (1 ea. = 5 oz)			6 ea.	$1.39/#	42%		
Onions (1 c = .66#)	3# 14 oz			$.35/#	89%		
Yams	4#			$.99/#	79%		
Cumin (1 T = .016#) (1 jar = 12 oz)		1/2 cup		$12.95/jar	100%		
Olive Oil (1 btl = 1.5 L)		1 1/2 cup		$7.99/btl	100%		
Fresh Oregano (1 c. = .20#) (1 bu = 4.5 oz)		3/4 cup		$1.99/bu	62%		
Garlic (1 bulb = 2 oz)	7 1/2 oz			$.99/bulb	89%		
Yucca (1 c. = 7 oz)		6 cups		$.69/#	90%		
Bell Pepper	1# 12 oz			$1.29/#	89%		
Jalapeno Peppers (1 ea. = 1 oz)			15 ea.	$2.99/#	60%		
Salt (1 c. = 102/3 oz)		2 1/2 t.		$.39/3#	100%		
					TOTAL RECIPE COST		

13. The vegetable served for a party of 300 will be a combination of sautéed yellow and zucchini squash. You are using the ratio of 2 parts zucchini to 1 part yellow squash and serving a 6-ounce portion to each guest. How many pounds of each must you purchase if the yield percent for zucchini is 85% and yellow squash is 95%? (*chapters 10 & 13*)

14. Your recipe for Coconut Pie yields 12 pies and calls for:

9 cups of shredded coconut
1 1/2 cups of flour

You want to make 26 coconuts pies.

  A. How many cups of flour should you use?

  B. How many coconuts should you order?

15. You have been asked to make twelve 4-ounce Kahlua Coconut Mudslides for a party you are catering.

Kahlua Coconut Mudslide
1/2 part Kahlua
1/2 part Irish Cream Liqueur
1 part Vodka
1 part heavy cream
1 part cream of coconut

  A. Calculate your cost to make this drink and the cost per drink using the following information:

$21.49/liter of Kahlua
$20.99/liter of Irish Cream
$19.08/liter of Vodka
$2.00/quart of heavy cream
$.99/14 ounce can of coconut milk

    B. If you charge $5.50 per drink, what is your liquor cost percent? (*chapter 14*)

16. A jar of dill costs $7.64. If the jar contains 4 ounces of dill weed, then how much will a tablespoon cost? (*chapter 7*)

17. A drink has 28 grams of high fructose corn syrup per serving. The bottle holds 2.5 servings. If a cup of corn syrup weighs 11 ounces then how many teaspoons of corn syrup are you consuming if you drink the whole bottle? (*chapter 14*)

18. At a winery 15 people are hired to pick grapes. They pick 15 tons of grapes which yields 1200–1300 Gallons of wine. (1 ton = 2,000 pounds) What is the yield percent on grapes to produce wine? (*chapter 6*)

Appendix:
Proper Measuring Techniques

Accurate measurement in the professional kitchen or bakeshop is crucial to recipes. In order to keep costs in line and ensure consistency of quality and quantity, ingredients and portions sizes must be measured correctly each time a recipe is made. There are procedures for using specific measuring devices that ensure ingredients are measured properly and with consistency.

Procedure for Using Volume Measures

Volume is the space filled by a liquid, gas, or solid. Volume measuring devices must be filled correctly to give an accurate measure. For liquids, use graduated liquid measuring cups or pitchers and fill to the desired level. The measuring utensil must be sitting on a level, stable surface for an accurate measurement. You should have the mark on the measuring device at eye level.

For dry volume measure, it is important that all ingredients be in the form called for in the recipe before measuring (i.e., ground, diced, chopped). Use nested measuring tools for dry ingredients measured by volume. Overfill the measure, then scrape away the excess as you level off the measure. Never pack down or tamp the ingredients unless the recipe specifically instructs you to do so.

Scoops, also known as dishers, are used primarily for measuring portion sizes of solid products such as cookie dough, ice cream, stuffing, cooked rice, and the like. When using scoops to measure, be careful to fill them completely and level them off so that each portion has been correctly accounted for.

Using Weight Measure

Weight is a measurement of the heaviness of a substance. In professional kitchens, weight is usually the preferred type of measurement because it is easier to attain accuracy with woeight than it is with volume. The tool used for measuring weight is a scale. There are different types of scales: digital scales, spring scales, and balance-beam scales. To ensure correct measuring, all scales must be on a level surface and kept clean and free of debris.

If you use a container or parchment to hold ingredients as they are weighed out, place the empty container or parchment on the scale and reset it to zero (known as tare). Digital scales have a tare button that resets the scale to zero. A spring scale will have a knob or dial to turn that will rotate the numbers or move the marker; in either case the marker and zero are in alignment when the scale has been properly tared. When using a balance-beam scale, place the container that is to hold the ingredient on the left-hand side of the scale. To zero out (tare) the scale, place an identical container, or an item that is the same weight as the container, on the right-hand side of the scale, and move the weight on the front of the scale to the right until the scale is balanced.

To weigh ingredients on spring scales or digital scales, fill the container slowly until the desired weight shows on the readout or dial. To weigh ingredients on a balance-beam scale, adjust the weight on the front of the scale by moving it to the right the amount of notches that equals the weight to be measured, or place weights that equal the amount to be weighed on the right-hand side of the scale. Add the substance to be measured to the left-hand side of the scale until the scale is balanced.

Answer Section

CHAPTER 1

1. **A.** 5/8
    B. 11/30
    C. 6 5/12
    D. 1 5/12
    E. 10 7/9
    F. 1/30
    G. 3/8
    H. 3 7/24
    I. 5/9
    J. 12
    K. 7 21/32
    L. 2
    M 2/7
    N. ¼
    O. 55/268

2. **A.** Too low
    B. Too high
    C. Too low
    D. Too low
    E. Too high
    F. Too low
    G. Too high

3. **A.** 1.5
    B. .375
    C. .5
    D. .3125
    E. .4
    F. .875
    G. .25
    H. .0625
    I. 5.2
    J. 6.6
    K. 4.4
    L. 4.4

4. **A.** 75.4724
    B. 1.0365
    C. 5.7019
    D. .2734
    E. 2247.8386
    F. .0002
    G. 2.2825
    H. .352
    I. .13
    J. 63

5. **A.** 72.85
    B. .0999
    C. .0025
    D. 1
    E. .005
    F. .25

6. **A.** 1.25%
    B. 999%
    C. .001%
    D. 40%
    E. 112.5%

7. 66.6%

8. 20%

9. 8 pounds

10. 204

11. 1000

12. 25

13. 165

14. 5.84%

15. .59%

16. 150

17. $117.60

18. 48

19. 20

20. 500

21. 48

22. 24%

23. 28%

CHAPTER 2

1. Volume measurements measure the amount of space the ingredient occupies while weight measurements measure how heavy it is.

2. **A.** A cup is a volume based on space and 8 fluid ounces is volume based on water.
    B. 8 ounces is weight and 8 fluid ounces is volume.
    C. A cup is volume and 8 ounces is weight.
    D. Water-yes, molasses-no, flour-no.

3. **A.** 16
    B. 4
    C. 3
    D. 2
    E. 4
    F. 2
    G. 2
    H. 16

4. 25%

5. 33.3%

6. Peck

7. Bushel

8. 6.25%

9. 75%

10. 18.75%

11. ¼ cup

CHAPTER 3

12. **A.** 32
    B. ½
    C. 8
    D. 16
    E. 128
13. No, don't do it, you need to weigh it!
14. When baking.

1. 368
2. 20
3. 358
4. 7.375
5. 19.5
6. 5.5
7. 40
8. 2.1875
9. 4.6666
10. .5
11. 22
12. 5
13. 1.1458
14. 12
15. 7
16. 57.52
17. 224
18. 224
19. 2.5
20. 300
21. 2
22. 84
23. .375
24. .1875
25. 1.625
26. 1.9531
27. 4
28. 1.25
29. 2.125
30. 4
31. 12
32. .9375

33. 13.125
34. 3.6875
35. 33
36. .00625
37. 6.4
38. 4
39. 4
40. 2.125
41. 27
42. 1.6

CHAPTER 4

1. **A.** 75
   B. 100

2. **A.** 5.375
   B. 7.1875

3. **A.** 16.0468
   B. 2

4. **A.** 3.125
   B. 20

5. **A.** 7
   B. 6

6. **A.** 6.125
   B. 4.25

7. **A.** 20.5625
   B. 3.1875
   C. 110.875
   D. 12.0625

8. **A.** 5
   B. 3.5
   C. 10.125
   D. 13.1875

9. **A.** 10
   B. 10
   C. 1.75
   D. 6.6406

10. **A.** 448
    B. 6
    C. 41
    D. 149.3328

11. **A.** 12
    B. .3125
    C. 56
    D. 3

12. **A.** 3.25
    B. .7968
    C. 37
    D. 3.25

13. **A.** 12
    B. 4
    C. 6
    D. 1

14. **A.** 3.4285
    B. 1.1808
    C. 4.5
    D. 6

15. 88.28%

16. 30

17. 2 tbsp plus 2 tsp

18. 89.5%

19. 9 gallons ¾ quart
    (answers may vary)

20. 50

21. 66 2/3%

22. 1.25

23. 45

24. 9.375%

25. .75

26. 1.05 pints

CHAPTER 5

1. 1 1/3

2. 5 1/3

3. 1.25

4. 14

5. 1.6875

6. 64

7. 3

8. .5

9. 1.3

10. .0833

11. 39

12. 9.4 or 10

13. 76

14. 224.6

15. 4

16. 6.4

17. 4.5

18. ½

19. 2.5

20. 1.4218

21. 100

CHAPTER 6

1. Good answers include leeks, juicing oranges, melons, pomegranate, etc.
2. Good answers include berries, grapes, whole baby carrots, grape tomatoes, etc.
3. 56%
4. 75%
5. 80%
6. 65.3%
7. 66%
8. 87.5%
9. 75%
10. 67%
11. 55%
12. 79.5%
13. 78.7%
14. 83%
15. Raspberries
16. Yield percentage is the percent of the amount that you purchase that you can serve. A chef can use the yield percentage to
    • determine amount to order
    • determine the cost
    • checking efficiency
    • determine amount that can be served
17. 39.7 pounds

CHAPTER 7

1. $.03 per ounce, $.34 per can
2. $.03 per ounce, $.44 per pound, $.71 per head
3. $.25 per ounce, $4 per pound
4. $.10 per ounce, $12.25 per bottle
5. A. $2.93
   B. $.62
   C. $.24
   D. $1.31
   E. $.71
   F. $.21
   G. $.24
   H. $1.42
6. $2.63 per pound, 32 steaks
7. $24.94
8. $10.60
9. $.15
10. $5.72
11. $3.71 per chicken, $1.06 per pound
12. $.36
13. $4.00 per pound, $.25 per ounce
14. $.72 per pound
15. $2.96 per cake, $.25 per slice
16. $26.94
17. $1.39 per pound, $.05 per portion
18. $1.99 per gallon, $.02 per ounce, $.13 per cup
19. $.27 per shrimp, $6.99 per pound
20. $9.34 per pound
21. $.26
22. $15.75
23. $.06
24. $1.46
25. $.56
26. $.40
27. $.28

CHAPTER 8

1. $.49 per pound
2. $1.41 per pound
3. $.57 per pound
4. $.59
5. $.42 per pound
6. $3.72 per pound
7. $1.60
8. $3.40
9. $.93
10. $16.51
11. $1.34
12. $1.11
13. $6.45
14. $.93
15. $4.21
16. $1.42
17. The edible-portion cost is always equal to or higher than the as-purchased cost because you have to buy more than the amount called for in the recipe in order to compensate for the trim loss when the yield is less than 100 percent.
18. The EPC and the APC are equal when the ingredient's yield is 100 percent.

CHAPTER 9

Page 98
1. $.42
2. $1.00
3. $.05
4. $.06
5. $.03
6. $.12
7. $.19
8. $.25
9. $.13
10. $.12
11. $.21
12. $56
13. $.05
    Total Cost: $3.19
    Cost per Portion: $.319
    Selling Price: $1.276

Page 99
1. $1.56
2. $3.24
3. $1.14
4. $.60
5. $.17
6. $.09
7. $.04
8. $.78
9. $.05
10. $.03
11. $.04
12. $.02
13. $.47
14. $2.75
15. $.57
16. $14
    Total Cost: $11.69
    Cost per Portion: $.7306
    Selling Price: $2.319

Page 100
1. $4.95
2. $.01
3. $.01
4. $.20
5. $3.00
6. $1.27
7. $.05
8. $.33
9. $.23
10. $.21
11. $.05
12. $.02
13. $.08
    Total Cost: $10.41
    Cost per Portion: $1.041
    Selling Price: $3.855

Page 101
1. $.45
2. $1.12
3. $.78
4. $.45
5. $.18
6. $.13
7. $.08
8. $.04
9. $.02
10. $.07
11. $.08
12. $24.30
    Total Cost: $27.70
    Cost per Portion: $2.77
    Selling Price: $8.15

CHAPTER 10

1. 32 pounds
2. 28 eggplants
3. 38 pineapples
4. 189 servings
5. 15 pies
6. 8 pounds
7. 17 pounds
8. 9 bunches
9. 8 pounds
10. 2 bunches
11. 10 pounds
12. 3 ounces
13. 5 pineapples
14. 45 bunches
15. 74 portions
16. 37.4375 pounds
17. 74 servings
18. 5,184 servings
19. 3.16 ounces
20. 48 servings
21. 93 servings
22. 44.7 pounds
23. 74 pounds
24. 86.6%, 58 pounds

CHAPTER 11

1. Yes
2. No
3. Yes
4. No
5. 52 pounds
6. 19 pounds
7. 10 pounds
8. 7 cases
9. 8 pounds
10. 7 cases
11. 22 peppers
12. 5 avocados
13. $.37
14. $3.99
15. $1.39
16. $1.20
17. $1.69
18. $.12
19. $.19
20. $.03
21. $2.00
22. $.03
23. $.03
24. $.63
    Total Cost: $11.67
    Cost per Portion: $1.167
    Selling Price: $4.67

CHAPTER 12

1. .3555
2. 2.5 cups
3. 2.6666
4. 1.17 cups
5. 3.125 quarts
6. 1.875
7. 18.25 pounds cheese and 1.75 or 2 ounces vanilla
8. If you make the recipe in its original form you are making 100 percent of it. To find 100 percent of something, you multiply by 1. Therefore, if you make more than 100 percent, you would multiply by a number greater than 1, and if you make less than 100 percent, you would multiply by a number less than 1.
9. The major benefit to using the recipe conversion factor method is that it saves time and it is easy.
10. The RCF is 18.
11. The RCF is .16.
12. 13 quarts plus 3.5 cups
13. Tomatoes, 11.875 gallons; onions, 9.5 cups; garlic, 2 cups plus 6 tablespoons; beef, 14.25 pounds
14. 4
15. 18.52 pounds

16. 2.5

17. A. 4.6875 ounces
    B. 7.5 ears

18. A. 15
    B. 1.4062 gallons

19. 6.25 limes

20. A. 4 tablespoons plus
    2.5 teaspoons lemon
    zest, 1.825 pounds
    onions
    B. 1.6 pounds lemons
    C. 2.09 pounds onions

CHAPTER 13

1. 7.5 quarts oil,
   2.5 quarts vinegar

2. 46.5 ounces oil,
   15.5 ounces vinegar

3. 2.8125 pounds sugar,
   8.4375 pounds flour

4. 20.3125 pounds rice,
   6.3476 gallons liquid

5. A. 1.17 gallons vinegar,
   5.25 gallons oil
   B. .5 ounce vinegar,
   1.5 ounces oil

6. 3.875 pounds carrots
   and 3.875 pounds celery

7. A. 21 ounces
   B. 30 ounces chocolate,
   25 ounces heavy
   cream, 5 ounces butter

8. 36 pounds

9. 22.5 pounds flour,
   15 pounds fat,
   7.5 pounds liquid

10. 3 pounds butter,
    1.5 pounds liquid

11. 15 pounds flour,
    10 pound fat,
    5 pounds liquid

12. A. 131.4 ounces milk,
    65.7 ounces egg,
    32.8 ounces sugar
    B. 128 ounces egg,
    64 ounces sugar

13. 12.78 pounds

14. 8 bananas

15. 9.89 pounds

16. Watermelon, 2.566
    pounds; bananas,
    1.924 pounds; can-
    taloupe, 2.24 pounds;
    honeydew, 1.6 pounds;
    coconut, .16 pound.

CHAPTER 14

1. 453.6 grams

2. 567 grams

3. 1.83 quarts

4. 35.27 ounces

5. 3.86 cases

6. 9 bottles

7. 2.94 cups

8. 101.4 teaspoons

9. 24.24 pounds

10. 1.417 kilograms

11. 6.8 kilograms

12. A. 12 cases
    B. $2.96

13. 2.5125 pounds

14. 6 glasses

15. 27 drinks

16. 695 drinks and $.83

17. 2.275 ounces vodka,
    .975 ounce Kahlúa

18. 1.25 ounces

19. 43% and $7.96

20. Liter bottles

21. 231 drinks, $577.5, 15.1%

CHAPTER 15

1. **A.** 5 cups
   B. 15 cups
2. .5625 cups
3. **A.** 70%
   B. 23%
   C. 76 glasses
4. 6 pies
5. 26 heads
6. 100% yield
7. Food Cost Form -
   Roasted Snapper with
   Tropical Tubers
   A. $43.52
   B. $2.61
   C. $1.53
   D. $5.02
   E. $2.22
   F. $1.09
   G. $1.72
   H. $4.18
   I. $2.02
   J. $2.54
   K. $2.81
   L. $.01
   Total Cost: $70.08
   Cost per Portion: $2.336
   Selling Price: $7.79
8. 2.916
9. 8.6 bunches
10. apples - 5.19
    pears - 3.83
    oranges - 3.5
    mixed dried fruit - .736
11. 8.11
12. 4.61 quarts and
    $.27 per serving
13. 88.23 pounds zucchini,
    39.5 pounds yellow
    squash

14. **A.** 3.25 cups
    B. 4 coconuts
15. **A.** $15.92 and
    $1.33 per drink
    B. - 24%
16. $.21
17. 10.77 teaspoons
18. 32%
19. $.26
20. $.03

Index

NOTES

NOTES

NOTES